PUBLISHER

İMMİB

İMMİB
(İstanbul Mineral and Metals
Exporters' Association)
REPRESENTATIVE OF THE PUBLISHER
S. Armağan VURDU, on behalf of İMMİB
HEADQUARTERS / MANAGEMENT
DIŞ TICARET KOMPLEKSI - A BLOK
Çobançeşme Mevkii, Sanayi Cad. 34197
Yenibosna - Bahçelievler/ İstanbul Turkey
Tel: +90 212 454 00 00 Fax: +90 212 454 00 01
www.immib.org.tr immib@immib.org.tr
BOARD OF PUBLISHING
**Tahsin ÖZTIRYAKİ, Rıdvan MERTÖZ,
Murat AKYÜZ, Fatih Kemal EBIÇLIOĞLU,
İsmail ERDOĞAN, Fatih ÖZER,
Ümit KOŞKAN, Muharrem KAYILI, Murat
TUNCEL, İrem UZUNÖZ, Buğra EROL,
Merve TAŞDEMİR**

PUBLISHING TEAM

**DÜNYA
ajansd**

MANAGING EDITOR
Gürhan DEMİRBAŞ
ASSISTANT MANAGING EDITOR
Eser SOYGÜDER YILDIZ
ART DIRECTOR
Hakan KAHVECI
NEWS EDITOR
Mehtap GÖRAL
GRAPHIC DESIGN
Şahin BİNGÖL
PHOTOGRAPHERS
Eren AKTAŞ
CONTACT NUMBER
Tel: 0212 440 27 63 - 0212 440 29 68
ajansd@dunya.com
www.ajansdyayincilik.com
CORPORATE SALES MANAGER
Özlem ADAŞ
(0212) 0212 440 27 65
ADVERTISEMENT BOOKING
Nazlı DEMİREL
(0212) 440 27 69
nazli.demirel@dunya.com
PRINTED AT
İstanbul Basım Promosyon
Basın Ekspres Yolu Cemal Ulusoy Cad.
No:38/A 34620, Sefaköy-İstanbul
info@istanbulprinting.com
Tel: 0212 603 26 20
TRANSLATION
UNIVERSAL DİL HİZM. VE YAY. LTD. ŞTI
(0212) 212 02 40
www.universaldil.com.tr

PUBLISHING DATE AND PLACE
Istanbul, Spring 2016

TYPE OF PUBLICATION *International Periodical
Kitchenware Turkish is published 4 times a year by Ajans D.
In whole or in part of any material in this publication without
prior written permission from Ajans D is expressly prohibited.
The written materials are the sole responsibility of each of the
writers, and the advertisements published in the magazine are
the sole responsibility of each advertiser.
A complimentary copy from İMMİB. ISSN-1309-4998*

kitchen_{ware} edito

Hello,

We are delighted to meet you once again at the International Home & Housewares Show 2016, in which we have participated for the 12th time. As İMMİB, we attend the fair with 13 companies on a total of 302.25 square meters in the north and south halls of the fair area. Cast iron, Teflon, enamel, plastic, melamine, metal, and glass kitchen, bathroom, and housewares will be displayed throughout the fair by our participating firms.

We are also together once again at the Hong Kong Houseware fair in which we organized a national participation for the 12th time as İMMİB. 23 of our companies attend the fair. Our national participation booths covering an area of 495 square meters are located right in front of the 3D hall entrance which sees heavy visitor traffic. The plastic and metal house-bathroom wares, stainless steel, cast iron and aluminium cookware and glass souvenir product groups are displayed in our national participation booths.

Let us take a brief look at the other titles we have included in our magazine, which we hope you will read with pleasure. İnoksan was the guest of our brand history pages in this issue. İnoksan has managed to be one of the countries that drives market share, that leads the sector, and exports by having a presence in the international market, since the day of its founding. Aykasa, Ayyıldız Export, Nehir, Kırteks Metal, Depa Home, Tekneci, and Yeşiller were other firms with which we conducted interviews. In our styling pages, we aimed to present you with the most original and newest designs the Turkish kitchenware sector prepared for 2016 and for fairs. We believe that these brand new products of Turkish firms will interest you as well.

In our nostalgia pages, we have taken a look at the art of telkari, which spread among Turks in the 15th century and thrived particularly in Southeastern Anatolia. You can read all about the fine points of this art that is particularly developed in Mardin and Midyat in our day in our magazine. In this issue, we heard the design stories of four designers who have made their mark with successful products in the kitchen wares sector, Ayşe Kırımlı, Ülgen Ayrancı, Berkan Kaplan, and Gamze Güven and the story of how they stepped into this profession.

Chef Gökay Çakıroğlu who was introduced to the kitchen at a tender age, and who is currently carrying out his profession at the Tapasuma Restaurant discloses the secret of cooking fine foos as "loving, loving, loving what you do." We conversed with Çakıroğlu on the profession of cooking, and we got his delicious recipes.

We hope you will enjoy our issue.
Until we meet at the Zuchex fair…

Chairman of Istanbul Ferrous and Non-Ferrous Metals Exporters' Association **Rıdvan Mertöz**
Chairman of Istanbul Chemicals and Chemical Products Exporters' Association **Murat Akyüz**
Chairman of Electrical, Electronics and Services Exporters' Association **Fatih Kemal Ebiçlioğlu**

turkish
kitchen
CONTENTS ware

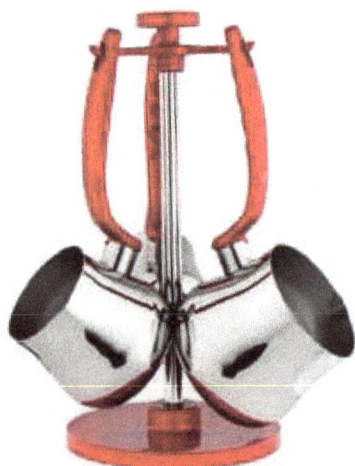

MINI BOX

MIDI BOX

MAXI BOX

ay-kasa ®

Folding Crates

www.aykasa.com.tr   info@aykasa.com.tr

We are looking for country distributors

LATEST NEWS FROM KITCHENWARE SECTOR •

CONTAINER WITHIN A CONTAINER FROM ARZUM

Arzum makes life easier for women with its Maximin Container Within a Container Chopper. The appliance offers convenient use in two dimensions with its large 1.5 liter container and its smaller 0.3 liter container for smaller portions. The Arzum Maximin Container Within a Container Chopper chops all types of vegetables and fruits without any problems thanks to its patented double tier stainless steel blade. It chops ingredients used in small quantities in dishes such as garlic with its small container while it chops foods of larger volume with its large container, thus preventing odors from mixing.
www.arzum.com.tr

KITCHEN SINK FROM ARTENOVA

The AE 850 sink model distinguishes itself with its convenient use and modern design. The product dimensions are 500 x 850 x 170. It can be manufactured as 0.60 mm and 0.80 mm at the ideal thickness desired. The product also comes with satin and decorated surface finishes. Since a siphon outlet can be used with a small or large whole, it is suitable for use with garbage compactor. AISI 304 18/10 cr.ni stainless steel compliant with European standards is used in the production of Artenova branded kitchen sinks. Therefore the products are offered with an indefinite company guarantee.
www.artenova.com.tr

DISAPPEARING FLOWERS AND BUTTERFLIES AT BERNARDO

Signing on a brand new social responsibility project with the principle of "respect for nature", Bernardo has prepared a special collection to publicize threatened species, in collaboration with WWF Turkey. Turkey's disappearing unique butterflies will henceforth be free in Bernardo's "Disappearing Butterflies" collection and the nearly extinct flowers will live on in the "Disappearing Flowers" Collection.
www.bernardo.com.tr

rengA

® ▲●■

new collection

2016

AMBIENTE 12 - 16 February 2016
HALL: 6.1 STAND: D10
FRANKFURT, GERMANY

IDEAL HOME HOUSEWARE 31 March- 3 April 2016
HALL:2 STAND: C01
ISTANBUL, TURKEY

HONG KONG HOUSEWARE EX. 20 - 23 April 2016
HALL: 3F STAND: F03
HONG KONG

ZUCHEX FAIR 22-25 September 2016
HALL:2 STAND C01
ISTANBUL ,TURKEY

MEGA SHOW HONG KONG 20-23 October 2016
HONG KONG

LATEST NEWS FROM KITCHENWARE SECTOR

VITAMINS COME OFF THE BRANCH TO TABLES

With Emsan's Multi Press Fruit Press fruit juices will come to your tables from the branch. The Multi Press Fruit Press that lets a minimal amount of pulp through, and has a steel filtration system will preserve your family's health for many years. The stainless steel wide container of the Emsan Multi Press Fruit Press can easily extract the juices of oranges and lemons as well as large fruits such as pomegranates. The Emsan Multi Press Fruit Press will add color to kitchens with its red, grey, cream, and chromium color and stainless steel color options.
www.emsan.com.tr

KAVSAN DOTTED TRAY

Kavsan which has 200 product varieties in its product portfolio serves with the manufacture of plastic, metal, wood, and ceramic products. Kavsan's product which is made of the union of two different materials will surprise you. The dots in the texture render the product skid-free up to high temperatures. This extremely durable, break and skid resistant tray is needed in any home.
www.kavsan.com

TEFAL INGENIO

All that is needed in the kitchen and on the table has come together in Tefal Ingenio with its high temperature resistance. Flavor will meet elegance, and tables will come alive with Tefal Ingenio. The Tefal Ingenio accessory set comprising a spoon, pasta service spoon, perforated service spoon, perforated spatula, ladle, slotted spoon, pizza cutter, can opener, apple slicer, grater, kitchen scissors, fruit-vegetable peeler, whisk, cooking tongs, salad tongs, mixing bowl and colander will add convenience and elegance to kitchens. Tefal Ingenio accessories that will be staples of kitchens and tables with their easily cleaned, sturdy, and durable design can resist temperatures of up to 250 degrees Centigrade, do not slip off pans and pots thanks to silicone rings, thus stay clean always.
www.tefal.com.tr

Gusto

KORKMAZ

Taste & Beyond

GRANITE

GUSTO, the biggest granite family which combines the greatest taste and design power.

LATEST NEWS FROM KITCHENWARE SECTOR

GROUND BREAKING INNOVATION FROM ARÇELİK AND SELAMLIQUE

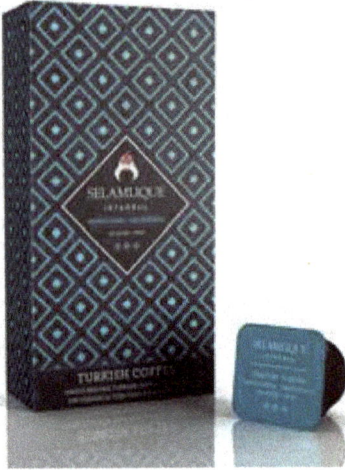

Arçelik, Turkey's leading company in terms of innovation, which makes a difference in the lives of consumers with the innovative technologies it develops, has signed on a brand new collaboration with Selamlique which produces Turkish coffee of superior quality in traditional flavor and various aromas, adding a brand new dimension to the customary Turkish coffee experience. The peerless know-how and experience in Turkish coffee of the Selamlique brand meets Arçelik's power in R&D and technology in the Arçelik/Selamlique Capsule Turkish Coffee Machine, introducing a brand new dimension to the enjoyment of coffee. Now, traditional Turkish coffee of excellent flavor is made ready within seconds, upon pressing one button.

www.arcelik.com.tr

JOY OF TURKISH COFFEE FROM TEKNECİ

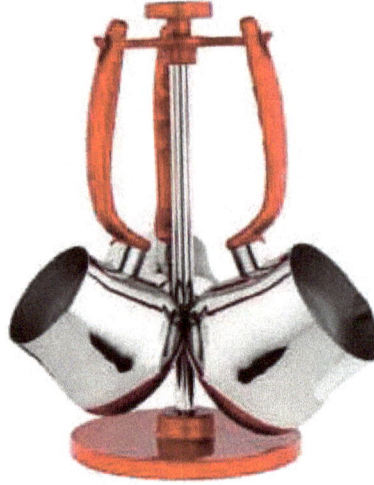

Tekneci Madeni Eşya with its 30 years of experience in the stainless steel kitchenware sector has managed to extend its market position in its own segment to a consistently wider area with each passing time period. Stainless steel coffee pots have carefully polished exterior surfaces that keep their shine at all times. Other features include: Ergonomic melamine handles that do not burn the hand. A wide base designed to prevent tipping over on stove tops. The choice of handle colors to suit your kitchen equipment. Wire or plastic hanger for convenient use in your kitchens.

www.tekneci.com.tr

VESTEL RED REFRIGERATOR

A+ energy class retro refrigerators offered by Vestel to bring color to your kitchen meet technology with different design with their versatile refrigeration system, odor filter, and wide volume. Equipped with a wide freezer the NFK510 puts an end to the problem of snow and ice generation with the Smart Defrost system.

www.vestel.com.tr

Mia Manolya

KORKMAZ

Taste & Beyond

GRANITE

Excellent scratch-proof interior granite and high temperature resistant silicone coating allows us to delicious meals with less oil. Recycable, entirely ecological, environment friendly materials are used for the production of Mia Manolya.

LATEST NEWS FROM KITCHENWARE SECTOR

ESER-İ İSTANBUL FROM KOLEKSİYON

Koleksiyon introduces the modern take of the first Ottoman porcelains stamped Eser-i İstanbul, which meet the quality of porcelain with a local aesthetic once again to your tables under the signature of Faruk Malhan. Inspired by the Anatolian table culture "Eser-i İstanbul" merges with the meticulous porcelain tradition inherited by Istanbul from the Ottoman court. Dinner, tea and coffee services manufactured with the quality of Bone China carry the new interpretation of tradition to delightful tables with their original lines, stark, gold, and platinum laced edges. **www.koleksiyon.com.tr**

THE JOY OF GRILLING WITH GRILL BORCAM

The Borcam family which are staples of kitchens and tables with their elegance and functionality continue to grow with new products. Borcam, the durable, healthy, and skillful kitchen helper now meets the joy of grilling with health with Grill Borcam. With Grill Borcam designed for people who do not compromise health and flavor, red meat, chicken, fish, and vegetables can be cooked with peace of mind.
Grill Borcam which was developed in three sizes comes with grill holes that ensure even distribution of heat throughout the food, where excess grease and juices drain and collect in the recesses at the side thanks to the convex design. The circular area at the center of the base of Grill Borcam prevents excessive drying, allowing the food to be cooked perfectly.
www.pasabahce.com.tr

KITCHENWARE OBJECTS FROM YEŞİLLER

Yeşiller Plastik has collected its kitchenware products under the Açelya brand. Açelya food containers preserve foods in healthy conditions for a long time while offering safe storage for all sorts of items. They are manufactured using polypropylene plastic. Their transparency allows you to see inside it, even when it is inside the fridge. Açelya strainer, dish dryer, and many other kitchenware objects facilitate your life while adding elegance and aesthetics to your kitchen with their modern design. **www.yesillerplastik.com**

Mia Manolya

KORKMAZ

Taste & Beyond

GRANITE

Excellent scratch-proof interior granite and high temperature resistant silicone coating allows us to delicious meals with less oil. Recyclable, entirely ecological, environment friendly materials are used for the production of Mia Manolya.

THE MOST ELEGANT GIFT FROM EMSAN

Emsan offers elegant, special, and convenient options from sets of pots to grinding mills, from mugs to sets of coffee pots. Emsan's mugs that will be used with great pleasure by those who wish to steep their tea in their cup with its porcelain strainer and lid, and its non-slip silicone base can be a warm gift alternative. Achieve convenience and elegance with the Dilan Coffee Pot set which comprises 4 pieces with red color options, the Verna Grinding Mill which will help you in grinding salt and pepper; and the Duracast 9-piece Hard Stone Pot Set that will be used with pleasure with its granite coating and silicone holder.
www.emsan.com.tr

A HARMONY OF COLOR IN THE KITCHEN

AN IMPORTANT PART OF OUR DAY IS SPENT IN THE KITCHEN. IT IS IN OUR POWER TO MAKE OUR TIME THERE MORE FUN BY ADDING COLOR TO THE KITCHEN. COLORFUL KITCHEN ACCESSORIES AWAIT YOU.

COLORFUL COOKPLUS

Colorful Cookplus products make your life in the kitchen easier. The Waffle Toaster offers a permanent solution in a single machine, rather than buying separate products for making waffles and toast. By changing the tray of the toaster, you instantly get a waffle iron. This machine is a candidate for the ace in your kitchen with its pink color, and its peerless waffles. The Cookplus Daily Mix rod blender will meet all your needs. Be sure to take a look at the pink colors of Cookplus blenders before deciding on a blender.
www.cookplus.com

MAKE TIME FOR YOURSELF

Korkmaz, which helps you make more time for yourself with the small home appliances it designs has a new product, the Mia Mega Blender Set that will be your greatest helper in the kitchen. The stainless steel set that comes with blending, whisking, chopping, and grinding functions can be used with convenience on hot and cold dishes. The product comprises four steel chopping blades, a wire whisk, a 1500 ml capacity chopping chamber and 1000 ml capacity measuring cup. The product which has a dual turbo speed setting also contains a stainless steel chopping rod and whisk. The product which has a non-slip surface also an easily detachable and washable mixing rod. The product comes in pink, lilac, turquoise, and blue colors in vintage hues.
www.korkmaz.com.tr

ADDING COLOR TO LIFE

The ceramic knife series is an Obje Plastik design which merges high technology with aesthetics. With its silicone coated ergonomic handle, and its ceramic blade which is 10 times as durable as steel, it is the ideal choice for your chopping and peeling tasks. Its 100% ceramic blade does not require sharpening, does not destroy vitamins, and does not carry odors. The grater with a polycarbon blade chamber is easier to use, healthier, and longer lasting than the metal graters to which we are accustomed. It preserves the nutrients of the grated fruits and vegetables, is easily cleaned, and offers health to your table. The Nar Tanesi is a super product that will help you remove the seeds of a pomegranate easily within a few minutes, and will make eating pomegranate fun.
www.objeplastik.com

EKBER®

"mutfakta herşey" 1977'DEN BERİ...

Türkiye İrtibat: İstoç Toptancılar Çarşısı 9.Ada No: 5/7
Mahmutbey / İSTANBUL
Tel: +90 212 659 96 00 / 01 Fax: +90 212 659 96 02
E-mail: siparis@ekber.com

International Contact: Firuzkoy Yolu Bağlar Mevkii Mezarlık Üstü Cad.
No: 9/11 Avcılar 34325 / İSTANBUL
Tel: +90 212 423 92 92(pbx) Gsm: +90 533 964 20 51
Fax: +90 212 428 17 58 E-mail: export@ekber.com

www.ekber.com

LATEST COATING TECHNOLOGY

Instead of common application on aluminium in the world market, Eternity shows its difference once again by using healthy porcelain enameled steel as a substrate for its unique production process. Whereas innovative 4 layer coating presents a healthier surface for cooking, it also provides a perfect functioning performance. As a result, the combination of latest coating technology and natural inspiration elevate cookto a higher professional level. With a variety of styles and sizes, you'll be sure to find a Granite Cooking Utensil that'is just right for you.

www.guzelis.com.tr

THE AGE OF GRANITE IN THE KITCHEN

POTS ARE KITCHEN TOOLS THAT ARE USED MOST IN THE KITCHEN. SINCE THEY ARE USED IN THE COOKING STAGE, THEY MUST ALSO CONFORM TO HEALTH STANDARDS. WE HAVE RESEARCHED GRANITE POTS, THAT ARE QUITE NEW AND HEALTHY FOR YOU.

THE HERITAGE OF NATURE

THE MARK OF "HASCEVHER" ON GRANITE

Exporting its products to 60 countries in 5 continents out of Kahramanmaraş since 1993, Hascevher using the latest technology with 850 employees, producing 40,000 units of cookware per day. Hascevher has the leading position in the copper, aluminium and steel kitchenware production sector. Today, the company aims to reach the same success in granite and ceramic kitchenware as well. To breathe fresh air into the granite industry, they have made this important investment. Their products include granite pots and They intend to work on different designs in order to improve their product range after the completion of this collection.

www.hascevher.com.tr

Jumbo, which adds flavor to dishes with its food preparation group carried this flavor to tables with new products. Turkey's first and only natural granite products are manufactured with the quality of Jumbo. Each Jumbo Doğal Granit (Natural Granite) product is unique, being cut from a single block of rock. Natural Granite products retain more speed than conventional pans, and preserve all the nutritional value and flavor of the food by giving this heat back gradually. Thus, the journey which begins in the kitchen with Jumbo preserves its flavor with in all its warmth on your table as well. Jumbo Natural Granite products comprise the granite grill, granite grill pan, granite pan, and granite pot.

www.jumbo.com.tr

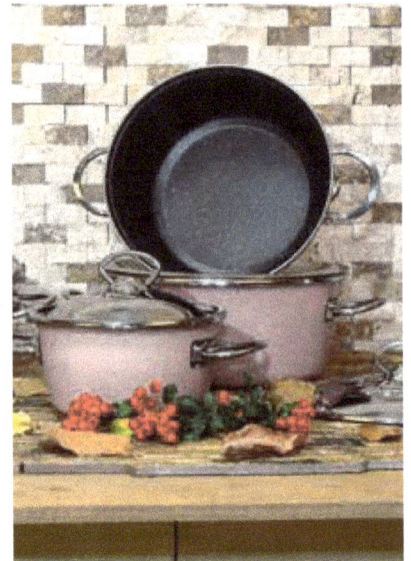

SOFT GRANITE SERIES

Savasan Enamelware has been in this sector for over 40 years and increased its reputation each and every year. Thanks to their R&D department, they have revolutionized cookware. Their products meets the expectations of the end-user not only in shape but also in the materials used for production. The Soft Granit Series was born of countless researches. It is heavy gauge and heavy weight, just like Granite stone. With the highest quality of nonstick coating, it is easily cleaned and saves precious time.

www.savasan.com

16

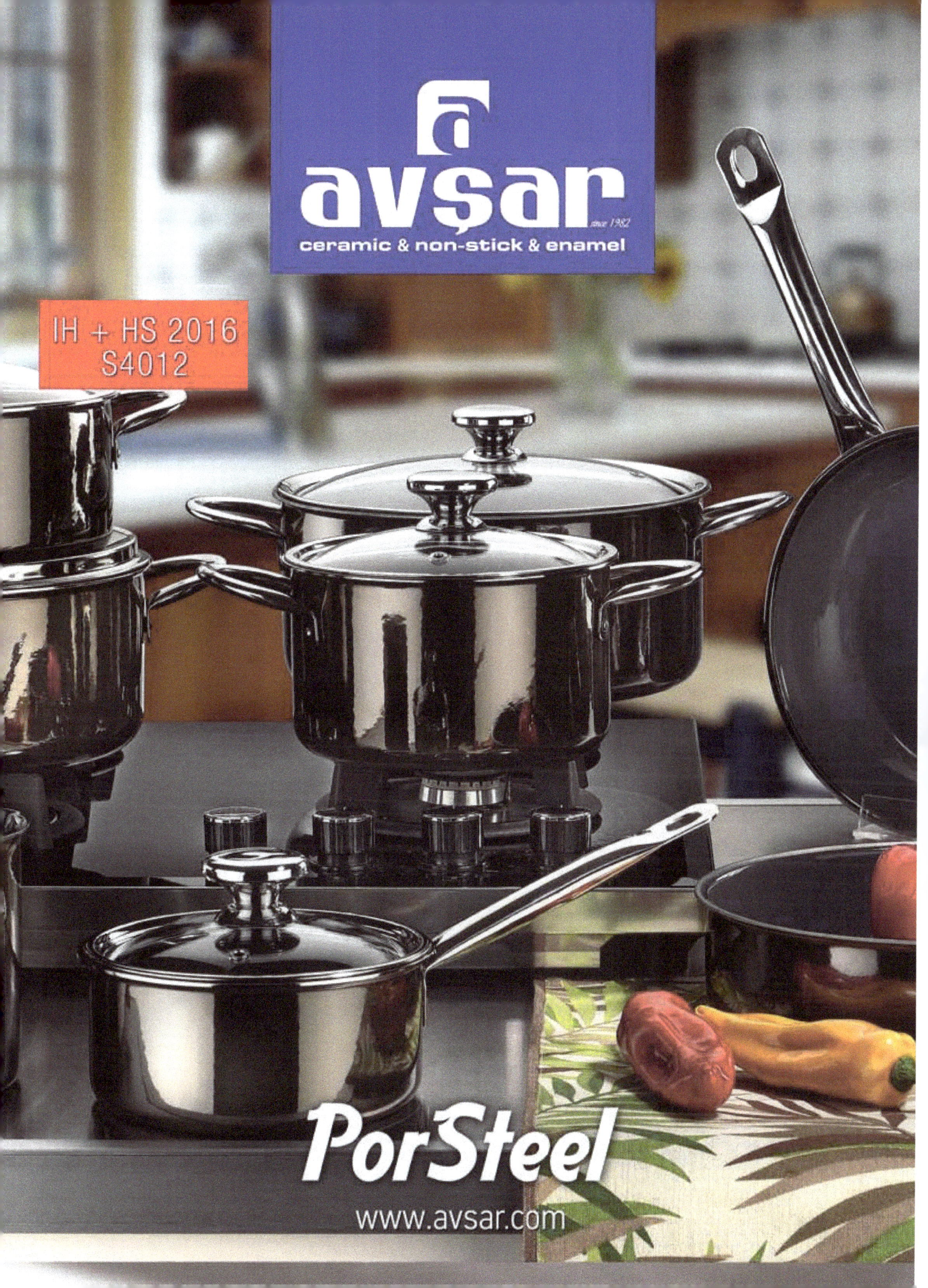

avşar
since 1982
ceramic & non-stick & enamel

IH + HS 2016
S4012

PorSteel

www.avsar.com

"A NEW INTERPRETATION WITH OUR OWN PERSPECTIVE"

Bekir Safa Yeşil spoke with Turkish Kitchenware, stating that they would be striving to open up to a larger number of countries in 2016.

How long have you been in this sector? Would you tell us briefly of your company's founding process?

Yeşiller Plastik has been operating in the plastics sector since 1972. We first stepped into the sector by manufacturing plastic barrels, and subsequently expanded our portfolio to cater to the bathroom and kitchenware sector, and we are still operating in this direction.

How do you create new designs? Do you have an R&D department?

While we create new designs, our principal concern is the pulse of the market. We also determine our preferences by considering demands and feedback of users. We keep close tabs on innovations and developments in our country and in the world, trying to bring a new interpretation with our own perspective.

Would you tell us of the investments you made in 2015? What do your plans for 2016 entail?

We have made efforts to expand our portfolio, for developing new products by making the needed additions to our machine park. We plan to continue

www.yesillerplastik.com

BEKİR SAFA YEŞİL, GENERAL MANAGER OF YEŞİLLER PLASTİK SAYS THEIR PRINCIPAL CONCERN WHILE CREATING NEW DESIGNS IS THE PULSE OF THE MARKET.

with the same speed and more in the same direction in 2016. We will be striving to open up to a greater number of countries.

Do you export, and what are the countries in your portfolio? Would you give us information about your export figures?

We export to many countries, mostly of the Balkans and the Middle East. Our export figures constitute for approximately 35 percent of our sales.

What kind of feedback do you get from fairs you attend?

Fairs are ideal areas for us to understand the positive aspects and

what is lacking in our work. Our perspective is to make good use of this feedback.

Would you tell us of your product varieties?

Our company has products in the bathroom, kitchen, and miscellaneous house wares concept, as Açelya and Serbas. In addition to these we meet the demand in an off-concept, but quite necessary area with the Açelya plastic lectern. In addition to having the first and widest portfolio in Turkey in the area of Serbas plastic floor treatments, we are a company that is popular in its sector and caters to a wide area including floor treatments for wet spaces, construction, pools, for jewelry businesses etc..

nehir®

www.nehir.com.tr

"WE EXPORT 80 PERCENT OF OUR PRODUCTION VOLUME"

www.aykasa.com.tr

HAKAN NİKBAY, VICE CHAIRMAN OF AYKASA POLIMER SAYS THEY MANUFACTURE CRATES IN DIMENSIONS VARYING FROM A VOLUME OF 4 L TO 45 L, WITH VARYING SYSTEMS FOR OPENING AND CLOSING AND ADDS THAT THEY EXPORT TO ALL CONTINENTS FROM AMERICA TO THE FAR EAST.

Stating that the folding crates they manufacture are the best in the world terms of locking systems, Hakan Nikbay answered our questions.

How long have you been in this sector? Would you tell us briefly of your company's founding process?

Aykasa was founded in 2006, as a subsidiary of the Ayyıldız Group of Companies which has a history of over half a century. Aykasa which develops its own designs and patents, brings convenience to people's lives in many places around the world.

Would you give us information about your production figures and business volume?

We work with an average monthly capacity of one million folding crates in varying dimensions.

How do you create new designs? Do you have an R&D department?

We have engineers in our R&D department, and companies with which we collaborate on a design outsourcing basis. Our new designs are formed with the perspective of producing solutions for market needs with creative ideas. I can say that we are the best in the world in terms of locking systems of folding crates, in particular.

Would you tell us of the investments you made in 2015? What do your plans for 2016 entail?

We have made many investments in 2015 in the areas of new product development and marketing. We aim to convey the convenience brought by our products to more users by attending overseas fairs in 2016.

Do you export, and what are the countries in your portfolio? Would you give us information about your export figures?

We export 80 percent of our

production volume. I can say that we export to all continents from America to the Far East.

What kind of feedback do you get from fairs you attend?

Fairs are very important for promoting products and firms. We seek the right business partners rather than direct customers, our most important priority is to work with the best suited distributor firm. We receive positive results in this sense.

Would you tell us of your product varieties?

We have products in varying dimensions from 4 l to 45 l in volume, with varying systems for opening and closing. We have 17 different products with active sales. We offer 25 color options. Since products are folding, they take up almost no space when not in use. All our products conform to food codexes. I could say they are very much suited for storing vegetables and fruits in the kitchen. They also keep vegetables and fruit fresh thanks to maximum air circulation. They are not damaged in any way by being stored in a deep freeze or refrigerator, or by high temperature.

Do you have overseas dealerships?

We do have overseas dealerships. We have dealerships in our retail channel, which also includes kitchen use. These dealerships were awarded to be exclusive in exchange for annual turnover commitments. We also have an agricultural channel, which is completely different. Distribution runs in a different way on that channel.

"EXPORT AROUND 13-15 MILLION US DOLLARS A YEAR"

EKREM KABAKCI, CHAIRMAN OF THE EXECUTIVE BOARD OF AYYILDIZ MUTFAK EŞYALARI TEKSTIL SAN. İÇ VE DIŞ TIC. LTD. ŞTI. STATES 90 PERCENT OF THEIR SALES ARE EXPORTS WHILE 10 PERCENT ARE DOMESTIC SALES.

www.ayyildizexport.com

We conducted an interview with Ekrem Kabakcı on behalf of Turkish Kitchenware who stated they have dealerships in Iraq, Iran, and Azerbaijan.

HOW LONG HAVE YOU BEEN IN THIS SECTOR? WOULD YOU TELL US BRIEFLY OF YOUR COMPANY'S FOUNDING PROCESS?

Our company was started by our father in 1975, by producing stainless steel coating. We manufactured the first baseless steel pot in 1982, and the first aluminium nail-on base steel pot in 1986. We set our course from production to active marketing in 2009, opening offices in Mid-Eastern and European countries, and proceeded to grow with our customers and employees without compromising on quality and customer satisfaction, and by constantly increasing our sales.

HOW DO YOU CREATE NEW DESIGNS? DO YOU HAVE AN R&D DEPARTMENT?

Since we make very frequent overseas visits, we create models that are current and useful in daily life in the light of our observations and research overseas, and customer requests, in collaboration with our R&D department.

WOULD YOU TELL US OF THE INVESTMENTS YOU MADE IN 2015?

As we know, our region has been going through a troubled period for the last few years. These political events reflect on commercial life as well. Considering these difficult conditions, we set our sights on different sectors, and entered the construction sector. As contractors, we are striving to adapt modern architecture to contemporary life and to be permanent in this sector.

DO YOU EXPORT, AND WHAT ARE THE COUNTRIES IN YOUR PORTFOLIO? WOULD YOU GIVE US INFORMATION ABOUT YOUR EXPORT FIGURES?

We export. 90 percent of our sales are sold overseas while the remaining 10 percent are sold on the domestic market. We work with almost all Middle Eastern countries including Iraq, Iran, Azerbaijan, Syria, Egypt, with Georgia, Greece, Germany, Morocco, Algeria, and Turkic Republics. We export around 13-15 million US dollars a year.

WHAT KIND OF FEEDBACK DO YOU GET FROM FAIRS YOU ATTEND?

Fairs have always guided us. We always take advantage of fairs in entering new markets, getting to know new customers, and ensuring product diversity.

WOULD YOU TELL US OF YOUR PRODUCT VARIETIES?

Almost all products in the field of kitchen wares can be found in our portfolio under our own brand. The predominant groups are steel pots, steel kettles, steel coffee pots, electrical samovars, Teflon coated pots, pans and etc..

DO YOU HAVE OVERSEAS DEALERSHIPS?

We have dealerships in Iraq, Iran, and Azerbaijan. We are working toward this purpose in some other countries.

"OUR EXPORTS CONTINUE TO INCREASE"

MEHMET FIRAT, THE OWNER OF NEHIR STATES THAT THEY EXPORT THEIR PRODUCTS TO CENTRAL ASIA, TURKIC REPUBLICS, NEIGHBORING COUNTRIES AND PART OF EUROPE.

www.nehir.com.tr

Sating that they modernize Nehir each year with new models and products, Mehmet Fırat answered Turkish Kitchenware's questions.

HOW LONG HAVE YOU BEEN IN THIS SECTOR? WOULD YOU TELL US BRIEFLY OF YOUR COMPANY'S FOUNDING PROCESS?

We have been in the glass ware sector for over 35 years. This process which we began by trading in Tahtakale has continued with production since 1981. We continue to operate with our nationwide sales and our exports to 13 countries. We continue our work without compromising on quality and aesthetics, in order to make Nehir an enduring and reliable national brand.

WOULD YOU GIVE US INFORMATION ABOUT YOUR PRODUCTION FIGURES AND BUSINESS VOLUME?

We have a monthly 1.2 million item manufacturing capacity as registered by the Ministry of Industry. We have an employment capacity of approximately 250 people including companies with which we work as suppliers and partners.

HOW DO YOU CREATE NEW DESIGNS? DO YOU HAVE AN R&D DEPARTMENT?

We work on new designs by keeping constant tabs on visual developments with our in-house staff of designers and engineers. We modernize ourselves each year with new models and new products by considering the needs of consumers.

WOULD YOU TELL US OF THE INVESTMENTS YOU MADE IN 2015? WHAT DO YOUR PLANS FOR 2016 ENTAIL?

We have added new and more powerful machines to our existing machine park in keeping with developing technology in 2015. We have completed the infrastructure needed for monoblock knife production. Our research and modernization efforts will continue with the same perspective within 2016.

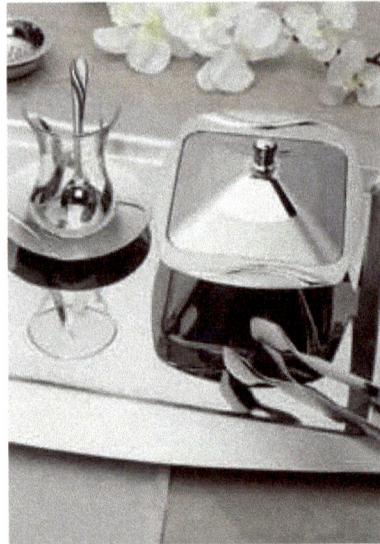

DO YOU EXPORT, AND WHAT ARE THE COUNTRIES IN YOUR PORTFOLIO? WOULD YOU GIVE US INFORMATION ABOUT YOUR EXPORT FIGURES?

Of course we export, and our exports increase every day. We sell our products to Central Asia, Turkic Republics, neighboring countries and part of Europe. We are making a serious effort to export to South America and North Africa within 2016. We are working to promote our products and represent our country with local and international fairs.

WHAT KIND OF FEEDBACK DO YOU GET FROM FAIRS YOU ATTEND?

The favorable opinions we get from meetings, and the interest shown in our products give us pleasure and pride.

WOULD YOU TELL US OF YOUR PRODUCT VARIETIES?

Although our main product group is cutlery, which are table top equipment, we also manufacture service equipment used in the kitchen. In addition to steel kitchen wares, our product range includes aluminium, granite pots and Bone China porcelain. All products which we produce and sell are protected by the quality guarantee of Nehir, and we desire to serve for many more years with the experience and stability we have achieved. We thank all customers, partners, and suppliers who have supported us through you, and offer Nehir products with our regards.

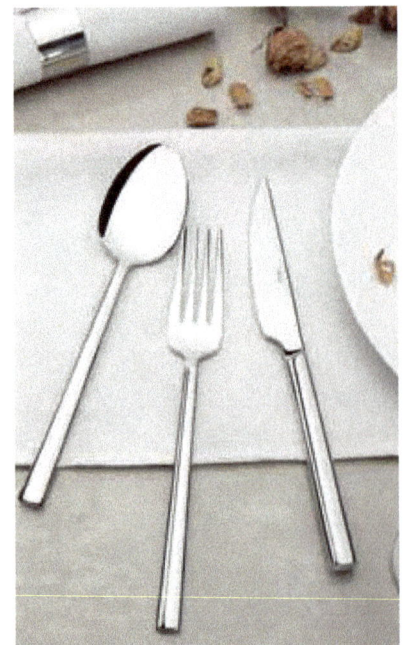

"EXPORT IS OUR PRIORITY"

OWNER OF DEPA EV VE MUTFAK GEREÇLERI SAN. TIC. LTD. ŞTI MESUT AKAN STATES THAT THEIR PRIORITY IS TO EXPORT TO FOREIGN COUNTRIES WITH HIGH QUALITY PRODUCTS AND ADDS: "FOR THIS PURPOSE, WE REPRESENT OUR COUNTRY WITH OVERSEAS FAIRS AND OUR EXPORTS."

www.depahediyelik.com

Mesut Akan stated that they export 60 percent of their production and answered Turkish Kitchenware's questions.

How long have you been in this sector? Would you tell us briefly of your company's founding process?

Our company which has operated since 1968 in Eminönü has enhanced its production of DEPA brand plastic products that has continued since 1983 with acrylic products in 2005. It conducts sales to the domestic market and to many countries around the world. As one of the first manufacturers in Turkey in the acrylic house and kitchen wares group, we aim to become a strategic partner for our customers with our high quality, reliable, and affordable products in accordance with consumer needs and expectations. With this perspective we improve ourselves every day in order to design and manufacture new products that facilitate life and that conform to international standards.

Would you give us information about your production figures and business volume?

We manufacture with consumption of a thousand tons of raw material per year. While 60 percent of this production is set aside for export, the remaining portion is sold to the domestic market.

How do you create new designs? Do you have an R&D department?

Products that will be manufactured in accordance with yearly trends are created by our design team according to their intended use and to prior market experience.

Would you tell us of the investments you made in 2015? What do your plans for 2016 entail?

In 2015, we have doubled our machine park. The 3D modeling department was established to issue the right products. The plans for 2016 include the addition of new equipment to our molding and production line in order to generate products for the new trends. We aim to complete these investments and installations by the end of the first 6 month period.

Do you export, and what are the countries in your portfolio? Would you give us information about your export figures?

Our priority is to export to foreign countries with our high quality products. For this purpose, we represent our country with overseas fairs and our exports. Some countries to which we export include Italy, South Africa, United Arab Emirates, Saudi Arabia, Egypt, Jordan, Qatar, Morocco, Algeria, Tunisia, Quwait, Greece, Azerbaijan, and Slovakia.

What kind of feedback do you get from fairs you attend?

Fairs are important for every sector. We get good results from the fairs we attend with our product diversity and service.

Would you tell us of your product varieties?

Our major acrylic products include thermos, tray, pitcher, glass, bowl, fruit bowl, spice sets, jar, salt shaker, platter, bread box, dish drying rack, cutlery holders for shelves and countertops, grater, egg cup, nut bowls, and chandeliers. There is also production in many other product groups.

"30 YEARS IN THE SECTOR"

www.tekneci.com.tr

TEKNECİ EXPORT MANAGER LEVENT AKMAN STATES THAT THEY HAVE BEEN IN THE SECTOR FOR 30 YEARS AND THAT THEY MANUFACTURE ON AN AREA OF 2500 SQUARE METERS.

We have conducted an interview with Levent Akman who stated that they manufactured coffee pots, spice cruets, milk pitchers and milk pans as Tekneci.

HOW LONG HAVE YOU BEEN IN THE PLASTIC WARE SECTOR? WOULD YOU TELL US BRIEFLY OF YOUR COMPANY'S FOUNDING PROCESS?

We as Tekneci Madeni Eşya have been in this sector for 30 years. During this process we have made ourselves a name in the Middle East, North Africa and in Balkan countries with which we have a joint culture by developing ourselves and constantly renovating our machine park. We have a manufacturing area of 2500 square meters as a company, and manufacture our products at our own facility.

WOULD YOU GIVE US INFORMATION ABOUT YOUR PRODUCTION FIGURES AND BUSINESS VOLUME?

We are capable of manufacturing 25 thousand sets per month.

HOW DO YOU CREATE NEW DESIGNS? DO YOU HAVE AN R&D DEPARTMENT?

We act in accordance with the demands of the market. We direct our efforts accordingly, and can produce new patterns.

WOULD YOU TELL US OF THE INVESTMENTS YOU MADE IN 2015?

We have assigned greater importance to exports in 2015. We will focus completely on export in 2016.

DO YOU EXPORT, AND WHAT ARE THE COUNTRIES IN YOUR PORTFOLIO? WOULD YOU GIVE US INFORMATION ABOUT YOUR EXPORT FIGURES?

We have only recently began exportation. We have recently exported to Egypt. But we can list the entire north Africa, Balkan countries, countries of the Middle East and the Arabian peninsula among our target markets at the moment.

WHAT KIND OF FEEDBACK DO YOU GET FROM FAIRS YOU ATTEND?

We have not attended any fairs yet.

WOULD YOU TELL US OF YOUR PRODUCT VARIETIES?

We manufacture coffee pots, spice cruets, milk pitchers, and milk pans.

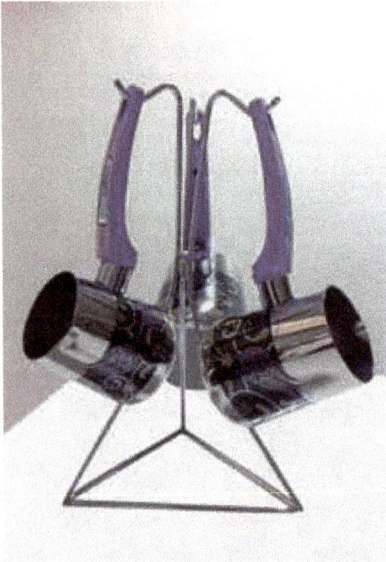

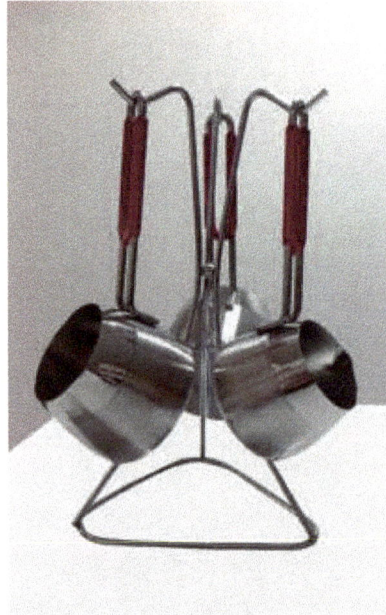

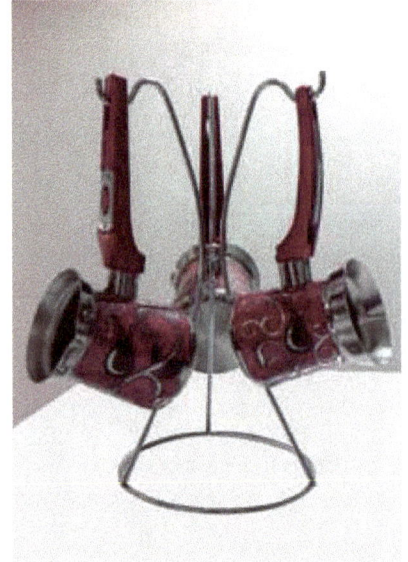

"210 THOUSAND ITEMS PRODUCED PER MONTH"

Stating that they export to Arab countries, Yusuf Özpınar answered Turkish Kitchenware's questions.

HOW LONG HAVE YOU BEEN IN THIS SECTOR? WOULD YOU TELL US BRIEFLY OF YOUR COMPANY'S FOUNDING PROCESS?

As Kırkteksmetal, we have operated in this sector for 25 years under the Akdeniz brand. Our company was acquired in 2011 by its current owner, Aksay İnşaat. We continue our production on an area of 24 thousand square meters in the Kahramanmaraş Organized Industrial Zone.

WOULD YOU GIVE US INFORMATION ABOUT YOUR PRODUCTION FIGURES AND BUSINESS VOLUME?

As Kırteksmetal we manufacture approximately 210 thousand items per month. These products are kettles, pots,

www.kirteksmetal.com

KIRTEKSMETAL GENERAL MANAGER YUSUF ÖZPINAR STATES THAT THEY HAVE BEEN MANUFACTURING FOR 25 YEARS, AND THAT THEIR MONTHLY PRODUCTION UNDER THE AKDENIZ BRAND IS 210 THOUSAND ITEMS.

pressure cookers, the non-stick group, ceramic, granite, teflon, and steel pots and handles.

HOW DO YOU CREATE NEW DESIGNS? DO YOU HAVE AN R&D DEPARTMENT?

We usually conduct meetings amongst ourselves for new designs and select new

designs by our own design team. We do not have an additional R&D department within our company.

DO YOU EXPORT, AND WHAT ARE THE COUNTRIES IN YOUR PORTFOLIO? WOULD YOU GIVE US INFORMATION ABOUT YOUR EXPORT FIGURES?

We export. Our principal countries of export are Arab countries. Egypt in particular. Naturally we target other countries as well. Last year we made approximately 10 million dollars' worth of exports.

WHAT KIND OF FEEDBACK DO YOU GET FROM FAIRS YOU ATTEND?

We can not say that we have a lot of feedback from the fairs we attend. We continue to keep in touch with some of them through e-mail afterwards.

WOULD YOU TELL US OF YOUR PRODUCT VARIETIES?

We manufacture steel pots, steel kettles, pressure cookers, granite, ceramic, bakelite, and handles.

DO YOU HAVE OVERSEAS DEALERSHIPS?

Our overseas customers usually purchase under their own brand. Thus, we do not have any dealerships.

ozti

IT'S TIME FOR
CAPPADOCIA

HOW WOULD YOU LIKE TO LEAVE THE HASSLE OF THE CITY BEHIND, TAKE A FAIRY TALE JOURNEY TO CAPPADOCIA WITH ITS UNIQUE HISTORY AND EXTRAORDINARY TEXTURE WITH A ONE HOUR FLIGHT? YOU CAN LOOK DOWN ON THE SPECTACULAR GEOGRAPHY OF CAPPADOCIA FAMOUS FOR ITS FAIRY CHIMNEYS AND UNDERGROUND CITIES FROM A HOT AIR BALLOON OR CAN HAVE A DELIGHTFUL TIME IN NATURE WITH SAFARI AND TREKKING.

Cappadocia has lately become a center of attraction for local and foreign tourists not only for its extraordinary natural beauty, but also for the alternatives it has to offer such as hot air balloon rides, safari, and trekking. Cappadocia which offers a wonderful option particularly for weekend vacations can be easily accessed with a brief flight from Istanbul and other cities.

Although Cappadocia which is one of the most important tourism sites of Turkey is known predominantly for Ürgüp, Göreme, and Avanos, the region has many other interesting formations and places to see. Wind, snow, and rivers have carved rock into various formations in Cappadocia that is famous for its fairy chimneys and underground cities. People have patiently carved the soft rock in the region, building themselves shelters and churches, and adorned the walls of some with pictures. Although Ürgüp and Göreme have become associated with fairy chimneys, 44 of the tourism income of Cappadocia has come from hot air balloons in recent years.

CAPPADOCIA'S CHARACTERISTIC HOUSES AND DOVECOTES

Since the stone, the only building material in the region can be easily processed thanks to its softness after coming out of the furnace due to the volcanic nature of the region, but it hardens after coming into contact with air, becoming a very sturdy building material. Since the material is plentiful and easily processed, stone masonry characteristic of the region has developed into an architectural tradition. The material for atrium and house doors is wood. The doors built with arches are adorned at the top with stylized ivy or rosette motifs. Traditional Cappadocian houses and dovecotes carved into rock manifest the uniqueness of the region. These houses were built on mountainsides in the 19th century. Dovecotes on the other hand are small structures built at the end of the 19th century and in the 18th century. The region is also famous for winemaking and grape cultivation.

You can not visit Cappadocia which is a wonderland with its subterranean cities, houses hewn from rock, and rock churches without also visiting the subterranean cities of Derinkuyu and Kaymaklı. You should ascend the Uçhisar castle and mount Erciyes and gaze down at the entire Cappadocia region. You should see the outdoor museum of Göreme to witness what mankind can accomplish. Do not return without seeing the Güvenirlik Valley and the Zelve outdoor museum. Do not neglect to see the Derbent valley, the Üç Güzeller (Three Beauties)

fairy chimneys, sunset and sunrise, and the moon at the Kızıl Çukur (Rose Valley). And most of all, do not visit Cappadocia without seeing Ürgüp.

DO NOT RETURN WITHOUT BUYING SOUVENIRS!

Souvenirs we encounter almost anywhere in Cappadocia include cloth dolls unique to the region, handmade laces and embroideries, marble figurines, various stones, model fairy chimneys, various copper ware items for the home, handmade wool hats, gloves, and socks in variouds colors, carpets, kilims, carpet bags, and hand-painted kerchiefs of Avanos Yahyalı.

Of course, there are also regional dishes you should sample. For example kebab cooked in clay pots, casseroles, Turkish ravioli, beans with pastrami, chicken cooked on a brick, trout cooked on a brick, sauté in fireplace and pitahs fresh off the oven are the region's delicacies. You can also buy dairy products, honey, yoghurt, and dry cottage cheese produced by villagers at the Ürgüp souk set on Saturdays. Large pumpkin seeds, potatoes, sweet white grapes and apricots are among other regional flavors.

"SPENDING TIME IN THE KITCHEN IS A PLEASURE FOR ME"

ÜLGEN AYRANCI

INDUSTRIAL DESIGNER ÜLGEN AYRANCI WHO STATES THAT SHE CURRENTLY WORKS IN A COMPANY WHICH MANUFACTURES SMALL HOUSEHOLD APPLIANCES WORKS IN THE SECTOR SHE LIKES, SINCE SHE ENJOYS SPENDING TIME IN THE KITCHEN.

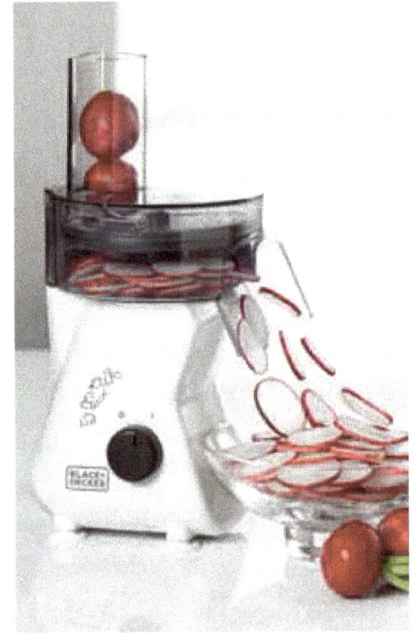

We have had an interview with Ülgen Ayrancı who says she has designed small kitchen appliances until now.

WHO IS ÜLGEN AYRANCI, AND HOW DID SHE STEP INTO THE WORLD OF DESIGN?

I am a graduate of the Industrial Product Design program of ITU. I love finding solutions to problems in daily life, and practical ideas. I have encountered product design as an area where I could do this as a profession. And so I chose product design since I thought I would derive great pleasure from my work. I have definitely made the right decision.

WHAT SECTORS DO YOU DESIGN FOR? WHAT IS YOUR PARTICULAR FIELD OF CHOICE?

I currently work for a company which manufactures small household appliances. Spending time in the kitchen is a pleasure for me, so I could say that I work in a sector that I like. My own experiences and my command of kitchen trends contributes greatly to my work. In addition to this, I also wish to contribute to human health by designing healthcare products.

WOULD YOU GIVE US INFORMATION ABOUT YOUR CURRENT WORK?

I have designed small kitchen appliances until now, and I am currently conducting a facelift study for a vacuum cleaner. I am being trained in mechanical construction (design engineering) as well as design at the company where I work, and carry out my own projects from start to finish. I could say that my workplace has been my second school in a sense. Aside from this, I participate in contests to see my creativity in various sectors. I most recently won first place in the İMMİB design competition in 2015 with my food container design which prevents mold, and has a measuring "spoon".

WHERE DO YOU THINK TURKEY IS IN TERMS OF INDUSTRIAL DESIGN PARTICULARLY IN KITCHENWARE?

Since I work for a company that has been doing this work for 40 years, I am employed in a more free environment as compared to other firms. Design awareness has begun albeit slowly to be adopted in our country. Differentation and innovation have become higher priorities for companies. I hope designs of worldwide fame will emerge in the years to come.

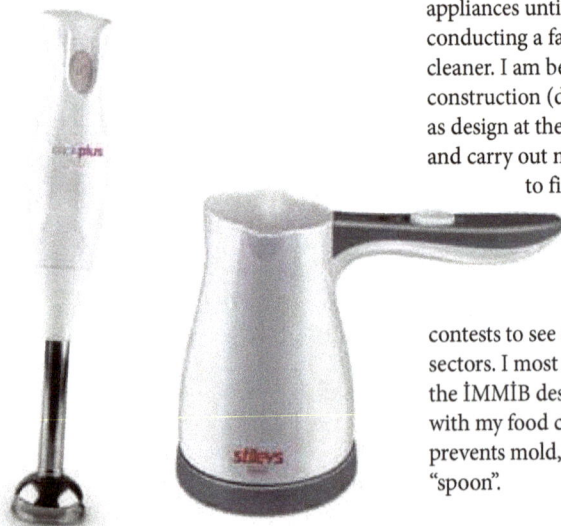

"MY AREA OF INTEREST IS PRODUCT DESIGN"

INDUSTRIAL DESIGNER BERKAN KAPLAN LIKES TO WORK ON ALL AREAS, BUT PRODUCT DESIGN IS THE AREA IN WHICH HE HAS THE MOST INTEREST.

BERKAN KAPLAN

Saying that the designer should create products in different areas to avoid becoming rusty, Berkan Kaplan answered Turkish Kitchenware's questions.

WHO IS BERKAN KAPLAN, AND HOW DID HE STEP INTO THE WORLD OF DESIGN?

I am a product engineer who has embraced the goal of designing the new and the better. I design products to make life easier for creative people who are always seeking for the new. After graduating from the Middle Eastern Technical University Mechanical Engineering and the İzmir Institute of Technology Design programs, I worked as a product development engineer, and design studio supervisor for 7 years in an international company (Ford Otosan). I have been working as a design director in Eksen Makine for the last 5 years. My entry into the world of design began as I tried to solve the problems in the products I used in my daily life, using my inherent creativity. This led to my progression from engineer to designer in my career. In addition to product design, I am interested in many different areas such as graphic design, fashion design, presentation design, and furniture design.

WHAT SECTORS DO YOU DESIGN FOR? WHAT IS YOUR PARTICULAR FIELD OF CHOICE?

I am currently generating products particularly in household appliances. Other than this, I work on many areas such as designing corporate identity,

website design, user interface designs, fashion design, outdoor cookers, presentation designs (porcelain, wood, metal), and furniture design. I like working on all areas, but product design is the area in which I have the most interest. But also I very much like doing graphic design work to regenerate and recreate myself. A designer should create products in different areas to avoid being rusty.

WOULD YOU GIVE US INFORMATION ABOUT YOUR CURRENT WORK?

You will see electrical tea makers, electrical coffee pots, and toasters I have designed for many companies on shelves this year. In parallel with these, my whimsical and modular furniture designs are also at the production stage under my own brand. Furthermore, barring any problems, the websites and corporate identity renovations of a very widely known firm will also bear my signature. We will be hearing the name of BerkanKaplanDesign outside the borders of Trurkey in the near future.

WHERE DO YOU THINK TURKEY IS IN TERMS OF INDUSTRIAL DESIGN PARTICULARLY IN KITCHENWARE?

I think that the sector has become more exciting and dynamic as some firms in the glass ware sector also added household appliances to their product ranges. We have many brands which offer products of a quality that can compete with the

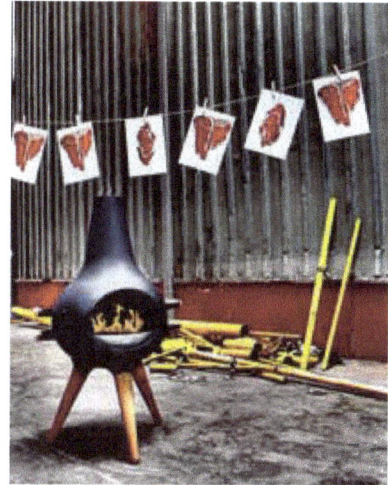

whole world. While design incentives lead producers and brands to receive design support, a fully efficient designer-industry collaboration has yet to occur. While very few firms employ in-house industrial designers, the culture and custom of working with freelance designers has not become exactly common. There are a lot of things to overcome in this matter. I think that designers who manage the creative process, which is a very difficult job are not valued as they should.

Design & designer

"DESIGN SHOULD MAKE LIFE EASIER FOR PEOPLE"

INDUSTRIAL DESIGNER AYŞE KIRIMLI SAYS THAT IN DESIGNING (A PRODUCT), SHE MAKES SURE IT SOLVES A PROBLEM AND MAKES LIFE EASIER.

AYŞE KIRIMLI

We conversed with designer Ayşe Kırımlı who relates that she had taken the first step toward establishing her own brand under the name of "AyseKrml".

WHO IS AYŞE KIRIMLI, AND HOW DID SHE STEP INTO THE WORLD OF DESIGN?

I was born in 1992 in Istanbul. I graduated from the Industrial Design program of Istanbul Arel University in 2014. I attended workshops taught by Gamze Güven and Ümit Altun, held in collaboration with İMMİB throughout my education. In 2013, I won 2nd place at the "creative design at the sales point" workshop that had been organized by POPAI. I worked as a designer at Mercanlar Mutfak Eşyaları AŞ between 2014 and 2015, and three of my designs are on the market. In 2015 I won first place in the Professional category of the İMMİB Industrial Design Competition. My lighting product "figurelight" that is inspired by the human figure was featured in the 42 Maslak "makingculture" exhibit curated by Ali Bakova and Gökhan Karakuş (Istanbul, 2015). She had the chance to work with Ali Bakova in the effective design in the kitchen project that had also been organized by İMMİB, designing the tea tray "Trio" for the Seden Mutfak firm, availing herself of all his experience and achievements from the past until the current day.

WHAT SECTORS DO YOU DESIGN FOR? WHAT IS YOUR PARTICULAR FIELD OF CHOICE?

While designing (a product), I make makes sure that it solves a problem and makes life easier. For this reason I do not discriminate amongst sectors. I create designs based on ideas I get or on the briefs I am given. My interest in kitchen wares has increased further with the experience I gained in the kitchen wares sector. I think I can design many products that can make life easier for the user in the sector.

WOULD YOU GIVE US INFORMATION ABOUT YOUR CURRENT WORK?

My principal goal at the moment is to develop myself in an advanced level by entering a postgraduate program. I have also taken a step toward creating my own brand, "AyseKrml". I want to be a name that is known worldwide by providing design consultancy and making more designs. I am also considering extensive projects having to do with 3D printers, that have become indispensable for designers in our day.

WHERE DO YOU THINK TURKEY IS IN TERMS OF INDUSTRIAL DESIGN PARTICULARLY IN KITCHENWARE?

Sadly, design does not enjoy the value it deserves in many sectors in Turkey. Most company owners base the financial value of the design on the resume and experiences of the designer without even looking at the design. This discourages designers that have recently stepped on this path. Particularly in an area such as kitchen ware that has a very wide scope, owners of all but few companies in Turkey avoid the risk of new products, preferring to manufacture existing products.

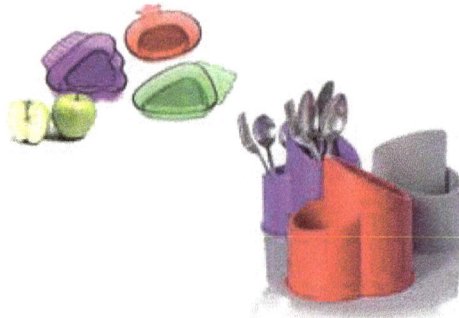

SHE BOTH DESIGNS,
AND PRODUCES

INDUSTRIAL DESIGNER BURCU BÜYÜKÜNAL WHOSE PRINCIPAL AREA OF DESIGN IS JEWELRY HAS MOST RECENTLY DESIGNED TEA GLASSES AND DECORATIVE BOWLS FOR THE PAŞABAHÇE OMNIA COLLECTION.

BURCU BÜYÜKÜNAL

We spoke with Burcu Büyükünal who is in the process of preparing for her March exhibit about her designs.

WHO IS BURCU BÜYÜKÜNAL?

I graduated from the Industrial Product Design program of ITU. After my graduation I began working with Ela Cindoruk and Nazan Pak's jewelry workshop. During the four years I worked there I both designed and produced. Then I won the Fulbright Scholarship and earned my postgraduate degree in the Metal program of the State University of New York at New Paltz.

HOW DID YOU STEP INTO THE WORLD OF DESIGN?

Soon after returning to Turkey I worked for Özlem Tuna for a brief period where I designed decorative bowls, espresso and coffee cups in addition to jewelry. In 2011, I founded the Maden Çağdaş Mücevher Atölyesi with my partner Selen Özus, and continue my work with my production in the area of contemporary jewelry and the training we provide on this subject. My most current work over the recent period are the tea glasses and decorative bowls I designed for Paşabahçe's Omnia Collection. This was also a return to industrial product design for me.

WHAT SECTORS DO YOU DESIGN FOR? WHAT IS YOUR PARTICULAR FIELD OF CHOICE?

I particularly work in the area of contemporary jewelry at the moment. I like working in this field.

WOULD YOU GIVE US INFORMATION ABOUT YOUR CURRENT WORK?

I am currently working for the contemporary jewelry exhibit I will open in March. Since it will be new work I do not wish to give out much information, but it has been a different approach than my previous work. I usually design and produce in the form of series. This job includes series as well but will also include individual works I have created.

MUSTAFA EMRE OLUR

"WE DESIGN INNOVATIVE PRODUCTS FOR FIRMS IN VARIOUS SECTORS"

INDUSTRIAL DESIGNER MUSTAFA EMRE OLUR SAYS THAT THE MISSION OF ALTERA DESIGN STUDIO IS TO DESIGN INNOVATIVE PRODUCTS AND TO FOCUS ON THEIR APPEARANCES AND INTERACTIONS WITH USERS FOR EVOLVING TIMES.

We spoke with industrial designer Mustafa Emre Olur about his designs and the culture of design in Turkey.

WHO IS MUSTAFA EMRE OLUR AND HOW DID HE STEP INTO THE DESIGN WORLD?

Basically, I love design... And for me, to love is to share. It was the beginning point of my design journey in 2003, after I graduated as an industrial designer from METU. With my designs, I do not only share a designed product, but also, my visions for a sustainable world and my scenarios about expected future.

With this design approach, I started to work freelance on industrial design projects with my current business partner Sevin Coşkun. In 2005 IMMIB organized its first design competition, where we received the second prize with a cutlery set and third prize with a cookware set, in the professional category. At that time, the culture and awareness of design, as well as the understanding of the definition of this profession was insufficient in the industries and winning prizes at a product design competition of this scale generated significant momentum and motivation for

our team. We continued to work freelance until we found Altera Design Studio in 2006.

WHICH SECTORS DO YOU WORK FOR? DO YOU HAVE A PREFERENCE?

Altera Design Studio is a multidisciplinary design firm, focusing on product, activity and space design. We work for firms in various sectors. We reconfigure the design process, from the concept stage to the production stage, according to the needs of each sector. In addition to our intensive work in the Lighting, Home and Office Furniture, Furniture Accessories, Building Components and Medical sectors, we occasionally design for Kitchen Utensils, Toys and Packaging sectors. We received a total of 24 national and international awards, including A'Design Award, Design Turkey Superior Design Award and Good Design Award, with our lighting, home and office furniture, furniture accessories and kitchenware projects. These prize winning projects increased our market recognition and therefore we mostly work in these sectors.

CAN YOU TELL US ABOUT YOUR ONGOING PROJECTS?

Right now we are working on two lighting product design projects simultaneously. One of them is a LED street lighting fixture for Arlight and the other is a spotlight product family for Lamp83. In addition to offering design and consulting services to firms, we recently started to get our own products manufactured. Tea, tea glasses and trays are traditional elements of Anatolian culture, which we reinterpreted with contemporary concepts such as speed, user-friendliness and sustainability, and created Spring. The production of this set started in February 2016 and it displayed at the Ambiente Fair 2016.

WHAT DO YOU THINK OF TURKEY'S POSITION IN THE INDUSTRIAL DESIGN SECTOR AND ESPECIALLY IN THE KITCHEN UTENSILS SEGMENT?

The culture of design is still in its infancy in Turkey, not only in the kitchen utensils sector but in all industries. Of course there are pioneering firms that manage to establish this awareness, employ in-house designers and/or acquire design services.

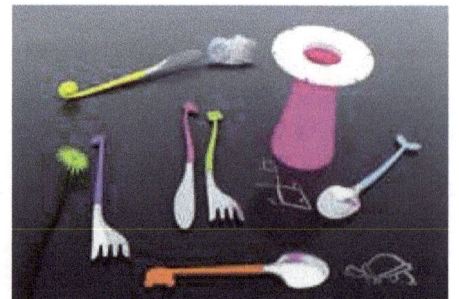

"THE SECRET TO FINE FOOD IS LOVING WHAT YOU DO"

We chatted with Gökay Çakıroğlu who says they strive to transfer Turkish cuisine to future generations by modernizing it by keeping basic elements in the forefront; and we sampled his delicious dishes.

WHEN AND HOW DID YOU FIRST BECOME INTERESTED IN COOKING?

In 1981, when I was only 5, I stepped into my profession without knowing as the youngest cook and mascot of the Mengen Cooks' Festival. I came to feel my father's profession of cooking became a feeling I lived in, as it would be my profession when I grew up.

HOW DID YOU DEVELOP YOURSELF IN THIS AREA? HAVE YOU RECEIVED ANY EDUCATION ON COOKING?

When I decided to practice this profession, I complemented my on-the-job training with a secondary education at the Vocational High School of Hotel Management and Tourism, and my bachelor's degree in Tourism and Hotel Management at the Republic of Turkey Anatolia University, taking sure steps toward becoming a formally educated cook. I also have journeyman's, master's, and master instructor's degrees for my

CHEF GÖKAY ÇAKIROĞLU WHO WAS INTRODUCED TO THE KITCHEN WHEN FICE, AND WHO IS CURRENTLY CARRYING OUT HIS PROFESSION AT THE TAPASUMA RESTAURANT DISCLOSES THE SECRET OF COOKING FINE FOOS AS "LOVING, LOVING, LOVING WHAT YOU DO."

WHEN AND WHERE WAS YOUR FIRST PROFESSIONAL JOB?

I began the profession in 1991 at the Dedeman Hotel in Gayrettepe, Istanbul, under the tutelage of my master Rafet Aydoğdu.

WHERE DID YOU WORK BEFORE TAPASUMA? HOW LONG HAVE YOU WORKED THERE?

In my youth I improved myself by working in such large five star hotels as Divan Hotel, Conrad Hotel, The Plaza Hotel, and after my military service The Marmara Hotel and the Four Seasons Bosphorus. I have been working at Tapasuma Restaurant within Sumahan Hotel since November 2012.

WHAT DO YOU THINK ARE THE BASIC ATTRIBUTES OF TURKISH CUISINE?

Our cuisine is like the story of an adventure from the past to our day. The Turkish cuisine which is one of the most developed cuisines in the world due to the long existence of the Seljuk and Ottoman Empires on these lands, and the long lasting control of Turks over the spice route, has many dishes and food types that can be a source of healthy and balanced nutrition in addition to their diversity and deliciousness. The diversity in the products offered by the lands of Asia and Anatolia, and the interaction with many different cultures throughout a historical process has ensured us a highly developed kitchen culture. And we are working to transfer this valuable cuisine that have been inherited from the past by modernizing it while keeping its basic elements at the forefront.

WHAT IN YOUR OPINION IS THE SECRET TO COOKING WELL?

Loving, loving, loving what you do…

Gökay Çakıroğlu

Lamb shoulder cooked on a slow flame

Ingredients:
2 lamb shanks (front leg)
200 g Medium size dry onion
100 g Carrots
100 g Celeriac
2 Bayleaves
20 g Fresh oregano
4 cloves of garlic
200 g of cornelian cherry
50 g of dried tomatoes
10 g pine nuts
50 g butter
100 g olive oil
200 g wheat

Preparation:
First marinate the lamb shanks in water that has been heated to 90 degrees and left to stand, by adding rosemary and orange rinds. Remove the lamb shanks from the water and lay them in a deep casserole dish with finely chopped onion, celeriac, carrot, fresh oregano, bay leaves, and garlic. After adding olive oil and covering with the marinate water close the lid, cook in a Rational oven under half steam, half bake format for 180 minutes at 165 degrees Centigrade, and after the cooking program has ended, the cooking process is completed by providing only heat for 15 minutes at 185 degrees. After removing the dish from the oven, let stand at room temperature for 30 minutes; take the shank out and separate the meat from the bone; garnish with dried tomatoes, sautéed pine nuts, and fresh spices, and shape using a mold. Puree the cornelian cherries and dab on the lamb; cook the vegetables left over in the casserole after draining the olive oil, making a lamb sauce by adding a little tomato paste. Serve on a round 32 cm dish with dried vegetables and keşkek.

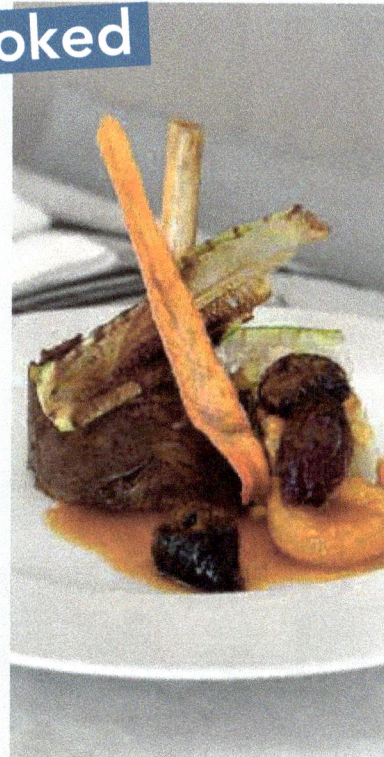

Sea bass with leeks

Ingredients:
Sea bass
200 g Dry onion
350 g Leeks
1 clove of garlic
250 ml Cream
400 g Potato
200 g carrots
One red and one yellow capia pepper
Squash 100 g Parsley, lemon, bay leaves, salt

Preparation:
For the fish marinate: Marinate the fish with bay leaves, parsley, salt, pepper, olive oil, and lemon.

For the leeks:
Julienne cut and sauté the leeks. Add bay leaves, salt, and pepper during the sautéing. Add cream when the cooking is nearly complete. Then place between two fish fillets that have been cleaned and de-boned. Then cook for 12-13 minutes in a 160 degrees Centigrade oven.

Potato cake:
Randomly chop potatoes and boil them in water for 30 minutes (until they easily break). Then mash them with a grater. Add chives, melted butter, chopped fresh oregano, parsley, salt, and pepper. Mix. Beat egg whites to a froth. Fold the froth gently into the potato mixture. Bake for 16 minutes at 160 degrees.

For the sauce:
Cook cream with chopped caper flowers, lemon, and chives. Serve with fish.

For the grilled vegetable tower:
Clean the vegetables and slice them to a half centimeter thick rings. Marinate with pesto sauce, grill.

THE NEW DESIGNS OF 2016

REPRESENTATIVES OF THE TURKISH KITCHENWARE SECTOR CONTINUE TO CREATE BRAND NEW DESIGNS AS ALWAYS. WE HAVE COMPILED PRODUCTS THAT WERE MADE IN TURKEY FROM A GREAT VARIETY OF INGREDIENTS AND OFFERED THESE FOR YOUR VIEWING PLEASURE. WE ARE SURE YOU WILL LOVE THE ELEGANT DESIGNS OF TURKISH FIRMS.

Ceramic pots **Hascevher**
Cake container **Zicco**
Servant tray **Lux Plastic**
Food containers **Gondol Plastik**
Lemon squeezer **Obje Plastik**
Glass water bottles **Renga**
Teapot **Özkent**
Cast iron pots **Lava**
Tray **Göreme Melamin**
Tray **Zucci**

Style

sty

Porcelain dinnerware
Bernardo

Spice jars **Eminem**

Cake top **Göreme Melamin**

Phaselis dinnerware
Kütahya Porselen

Neptün pot **Emsan**

Lizbon coffee pots **Hisar**

Food containers **Zucci**

Ceramic pots
Hascevher

London porcelain dinnerware
Jumbo

Colander
Gondol Plastik

sty

Dream collection **Korkmaz**

Mitterteich collection **Kütahya Porselen**

Molds **Lux Plastic**

Didim cutlery **Hisar**

Destina icecream bowl **Lav**

Teapot **Özkent**

Porcelain dinnerware **Porland**

Food containers **Obje Plastik**

Glassware **Paşabahçe**

Rose garden collection
Jumbo

turkish kitchenware style

Ceramic dinneware **SNT**

Water bottles **Renga**

Toaster **Lava**

Feelsteelcam kettle **Emsan**

2016 NEW COLLECTION

VIOLET house®

Turkey KASTAMONU PLASTIK SANAYI
www.kastamonuplastik.com.tr

Dantela Products

"İNOKSAN IS A TURKISH BRAND WHICH DRAWS THE WORLD'S INTEREST"

Vehbi Varlık states that İnoksan allocates 2 percent of its annual turnover to R&D, and that a staff of 20 works to develop new products in the R&D department, and adds that they had developed 6 patented, 7 beneficial models and 22 design registered works as a result of these efforts.

How would you like to become more closely acquainted with İnoksan? Would you tell us briefly of your company's founding process?

Our company which celebrates its 35th anniversary in the industrial kitchen equipments sector has developed many pioneering works to date, and offered its innovative products for the use of its customers. We manufacture for our customers based not only in Turkey, but in a wide geography worldwide, at our factory in Bursa, which has been equipped as a state-of-the-art industrial base on an indoor area of 20,000 square meters. Today, İnoksan is a Turkish brand which draws the world's interest. In this aspect, it distinguishes itself from its competitors. İnoksan has managed to be one of the countries that drives market share, that leads the sector, and exports by having a presence in the international market, since the day of its founding. As İnoksan, we ascribe great importance to technology in industrial kitchen equipment. As required by our customer-oriented approaches, we implement fast, high quality, and low cost manufacturing, and support our products with advanced technology machinery and equipment.

How do you create new designs? Do you have a R&D department?

R&D is among the areas in which İnoksan invests the most. The company allocates 2 percent of its turnover to

VEHBİ VARLIK
CHAIRMAN OF THE
EXECUTIVE BOARD

R&D every year. A staff of 20 works to develop new products at the İnoksan R&D department. 6 patented, 7 beneficial models and 22 design registered works have been developed to date as a result of these efforts. As İnoksan, we ascribe great importance to technology. As required by our customer-oriented approach, we implement fast, high quality, and low cost manufacturing, and support our products with advanced technology machinery and equipment. We continue these efforts with our staff of 12 people in total, including 4

bachelor's of degree and 1 master's degree holders, and 1 postgraduate students in our R&D department. Our immediate objective is to increase the number of staff of our R&D department to 30 and above and to employ people equipped with high qualifications and design skills in this department. As a result of these efforts, we aim to be an R&D center registered by the Ministry of Technology.

Would you tell us of the investments you made in 2015?

Throughout 2015 we have invested in "increasing quality", "removing bottlenecks" and "developing technology" in the manufacturing side. We have started to use robot source technologies in the production of industrial kitchen equipment. We have invested in additional machinery and equipment in sections of heavy and slowed manufacturing flow, making these sections faster. Aside from these, we have manufactured new products that offer ergonomics, economy, and aesthetic advantages and offered them for the enjoyment of our customers.

DO YOU EXPORT, AND WHAT ARE THE COUNTRIES IN YOUR PORTFOLIO? WOULD YOU GIVE US INFORMATION ABOUT YOUR EXPORT FIGURES?

As İnoksan, we serve both local and overseas markets. We export İnoksan products to 66 countries on 5 continents. We have a turnover of over TRY 130 million at our factory which has been transformed into an industrial base equipped with state-of-the-art technology, and export 35% of our production. As Russia, Turkic Republics, Iran, Iraq, Jordan, and Saudi Arabia take center stage in regional markets, Italy and Germany in the European Union, and the US, Mexico, Brazil, and Chile on the American Continents are other markets we focus on. North African and other African countries will continue to be our focal point in project based sales.

WHAT KIND OF FEEDBACK DO YOU GET FROM FAIRS YOU ATTEND?

We offer the kitchens the quality they deserve not only in Turkey, but in various countries of the world. In this context, we keep close tabs on the important fairs of the sector, and promote our quality to the world. As we inform our customers about the latest developments regarding our company, we offer our conventional and latest products together to fair visitors. As İnoksan, we have attended the Pir, NRA, Ibatech, and Host Milano fairs in 2015.

WOULD YOU TELL US OF YOUR PRODUCT VARIETIES?

While our main area of operation in İnoksan is the industrial kitchen sector, we have solution partnerships with turnkey projects in the areas of launderette, cold room, open buffet, and service lines. The products we manufacture for the industrial kitchen sector include Cooking Applicances and Equipments, Dishwasher Equipment, İnoksdesign (Open Buffet and Service Lines), Food Preparation Machines, Hoods – Floor Grilles – Grease Eliminators,–Storage and Stacking Units, Coolers, Ship's Galleys, Service Carts and Launderette Machinery and Equipment. Ice machines, meat chopping machines, food slicing machines, garbage grinders, dough rolling and citrus squeezing machines are also included in our portfolio under the category of Imported Products. As İnoksan, we have products catering to specific areas such as launderettes, and ship's galleys, with industrial equipment being at the forefront.

DO YOU HAVE OVERSEAS DEALERSHIPS?

As İnoksan, we have been exporting since 1986. Our first overseas dealership began operations in 1993, and we continue our sales with 73 dealers in 80 countries.

WHAT DO YOUR PLANS FOR 2016 ENTAIL?

We aim to grow by another 15 percent in 2016. Aside from our growth objective, we also have internal transformation objectives. We also aim to raise the share

of exports in our turnover to 50%. We are moving on various indicators, led by overseas market diversification and adding replacement markets for risky markets, new technological product launches, and increasing our share in the healthcare market. We aim to once again make the highest investment in 2016 in R&D and human resources. Aside from these, we will invest in increased capacity on the Cooler, Oven, and Dishwasher lines. We will be in the market with energy efficiency-oriented R&D efforts and products reflecting ergonomic-oriented designs in 2016. We believe that we will make our mark in the industrial kitchen sector in the year to come with our self-cleaning Combination ovens, dishwashers with a capacity of washing 7,000 dishes an hour, and our newly designed Coolers.

WHICH OF YOUR PRODUCTS DID CONSUMERS PREFER MOST IN 2014-2015?

In 2014 and 2015, our most popular products were our new technology ovens, dishwashers, and coolers. Aside from these, our storage and stacking units as well as our food preparation and service equipment were also popular products.

WHAT DO YOU CONSIDER WHILE PREPARING YOUR PRODUCT PORTFOLIO?

We offer 10 to 20 new products to the market each year. At the end of each year products are examined, and those products that will be removed from the product portfolio and the new products that will be included in the portfolio are determined. Therefore while new products are added to the product portfolio each year, there are others that are removed. The feedback we receive from our customers is very important at this point. We heed the voice of our existing and potential customers, and create our product portfolio on the basis of their comments. The comments and assessments received from customers also guide our innovation and R&D efforts. We manage our R&D efforts to meet the needs and expectations of our sector and our customers.

THE ART OF WIRE:
TELKARI

THE ART OF TELKARI, WHICH SPREAD AMONG TURKS IN THE 15TH CENTURY AND THRIVED PARTICULARLY IN SOUTHEASTERN ANATOLIA IS DEVELOPED TODAY ESPECIALLY IN MARDIN AND MIDYAT. JEWELRY BOXES, CHANDELIERS, TRAYS, SUGAR BOWLS, VASES, MOUTHPIECES, AND JEWELRY ARE CRAFTED USING THE METHOD OF TELKARI WHICH IS A DIFFICULT AND PAINSTAKING CRAFT, AND ONE THAT IS TAUGHT BY A MASTER TO AN APPRENTICE.

It is claimed that the first address of metalworking is Anatolia. Decorative objects made of copper and lead, unearthed in excavations in Çatalhöyük reinforce the thesis that this art has a history longer than 8000 years. Gold, silver, copper, brass, and bronze objects of traditional Turkish mine craft are the works of Seljuk and Ottoman masters. The art of jewelry making where gold and silver are used as principal materials has a privileged place in Turkish metalworking. According to findings obtained from archeological digs, it is

WHAT IS TELKARI?

Telkari is the name given to the art of working gold and silver filigree. The dictionary meaning of the word telkari is "the art performed with wire". Telkari, which has a special place among traditional handicrafts is a symbol of the beauty, aesthetics, and elegance of the decorative approach in Turkish culture. It is the working of gold and silver wires, that are as thin as a strand of hair, as it were. The fineness of the art which is prominent in products worked with telkari, the jewelry adorned with patterns, and decorative products for the home add color to the lives of their owners with their delicacy and their value. Like all Ottoman arts, telkari is a difficult, painstaking art that is taught by a master to his apprentice.

understood that the technique of telkari has been used in Mesopotamia since 3000 BC, and in Anatolia since 2500 BC. It is known that the art of telkari was common amongst Turks since the 15th century, and was highly developed particularly in Southeastern Anatolia.

The masters of the art whose living area began to be constricted due to the industrialization in the jewelry sector have managed to carry the art of telkari to our day. The art is particularly developed in the province of Mardin and its district of Mardin. In fact Mardin and its district of Midyat have already taken their place in memory as the place where telkari was born and where it flourished. Masters of the art whose current numbers can be counted with one hand continue to work keep the art alive and to sustain it into the future.

PAINSTAKING WORK

As is the case in many of our traditional arts, the artist must produce all materials he will use in his work by himself. Silver ingots or silver scraps are melted in a crucible and cast into thin rods. These rods are then passed through cylinders and rods until they reach the thickness desired. The product that will be created is first drawn on paper in 1/1 scale. The wires are frequently tempered as they are drawn and worked into the product. The cut and flattened parts of the main framework of the product are laid and shaped on the drawn pattern and joined in certain places by welding. Then the framework is completed by adding the thin wires. The empty sections within the framework are filled in with thinner wires and compressed, and welded where necessary. Each of the parts that have been thus prepared by filling in with wires are given their final shape by bending or pitting and the parts are brought together by adding connecting elements.

WHAT KIND OF PRODUCTS ARE MADE OF TELKARI?

Covers for lighters, cigarette and jewelry boxes, chandeliers, trays, sugar bowls, vases, mouthpieces, covers for pitchers and other objects, lamp shades, earrings, headpieces, necklaces, bracelets, belts, rings, spoon holders, prayer beads, and ashtrays.

turkish
kitchen
ware

INTERNATIONAL HOME & HOUSEWARESSHOW 2016

The national participation of Turkey in the International Home & Housewares Show 2016 held in Chicago, U.S. between 5-8 March 2016, and recognized as one of the most important fairs in the sector with regard to house wares, kitchen wares, and cooking equipment is being organized by IMMIB (Istanbul Minerals and Metals Exporter's Associations) for the 12th time this year. İMMİB will attend the fair with 13 companies on a total of 302.25 square meters in the north and south halls of the fair area. Cast iron, Teflon, enamel, plastic, melamine, metal, and glass kitchen, bathroom, and house wares will be displayed throughout the fair by our participating firms.

THE HONG KONG HOUSEWARE 2016 FAIR

This year, 23 firms participate in the Hong Kong Houseware fair, for which İMMİB has organized Turkey's national participation for the 12th time between April 20-23, 2016. Our national participation booths covering an area of 495 square meters will be located right in front of the 3D hall entrance which sees heavy visitor traffic. The plastic and metal hose-bathroom wares, stainless steel, cast iron and aluminum cookware and glass souvenir product groups will be displayed in our national participation booths.

For colorful kitchens

NOUVAL

NOUVAL GROUP MUTFAK EŞYALARI DIŞ TİC. LTD. ŞTİ.

THE SECOND INSTANCE OF THE TURKISH HOUSEWARES UR-GE PROJECT TRAINING WAS HELD

Following the first training held in December within the scope of the Turkish Housewares UR-GE (Support of the Development of International Competition) project held for the benefit of the Turkish house and kitchen wares sector, by the Istanbul Chemicals and Chemical Products Exporters' Association (İKMİB), in collaboration with the Home and Kitchen Appliances Industrialists and Exporters Association (EVSİD); the "Corporate Performance Measurement Systems Management" training that had been selected as the second training event was held at the Foreign Trade Complex and EVSİD offices between 13th and 14th of January by the Rönesans company.

VISITS TO INDONESIA AND VIETNAM WITHIN THE SCOPE OF UR-GE

A visit will be made by the commercial delegation to Jakarta/Indonesia and HoChiMinh/Vietnam between the 20th and 27th of March, 2016 with the attendance of cluster companies, within the scope of the the first stage of the Turkish Housewares UR-GE (Support of the Development of International Competition) project held for the benefit of the household and kitchen wares sector by the Istanbul Chemicals and Chemical Products Exporters' Association (İKMİB), in collaboration with the Home and Kitchen Appliances Industrialists and Exporters Association (EVSİD).

Indonesia which imports 237 million dollars' worth of kitchen wares as of 2014 has increased its demand for high quality items in parallel with its developing population and the rise in its average income level, becoming a significant market for the manufacturers of Turkey. And unlike the common perception, Vietnam which similarly imports kitchen wares in the amount of 122 million dollars imports a significant amount of high quality kitchen wares in addition to cheap Far Eastern products. While Vietnam imported 11 million dollars' worth of goods from Japan, and 2,1 million dollars' worth from Germany only imported 420 thousand dollars' worth of goods from Turkey.

Within this framework, the overseas marketing event which will encompass the cities of Jakarta, the capital of Indonesia, and HoChiMinh, the commercial center of Vietnam and include an examination of the distribution channels in both countries and one on one business interviews with potential buyers will make positive contributions to the sector's exports to said countries.

CONTACTFILE

TURKISH KITCHENWARE EXPORTERS

KITCHENWARE ●
PLASTICWARE ●
ELECTRICAL ●
INDUSTRIAL ●
TABLEWARE ●
GIFTWARE ●
HOUSEWARE ●

FOR MORE INFORMATION ABOUT
TURKISH KITCHENWARE, PLEASE CONTACT US
bugra.erol@immib.org.tr

iMMiB

İSTANBUL MINERAL AND METALS EXPORTERS' ASSOCIATION
Dış Ticaret Kompleksi-A Blok Çobançeşme Mevkii, Sanayi Cad. 34197 Yenibosna Bahçelievler - İstanbul
TURKEY Tel: +90 212 454 00 00 Fax: +90 212 454 00 01 e-mail: immib@immib.org.tr www.immib.org.tr

HOUSEWARE · GIFTWARE · TABLEWARE · INDUSTRIAL · ELECTRICAL · PLASTICWARE · KITCHENWARE

3-D THE GLASSWARE COMPANY
Tel: +90 216 583 04 70 Fax: +90 216 583 04 81
Web: www.3dglassware.come-mail: info@3dglassware.com

AB-KA KRİSTAL DECORATED GLASSWARE
Tel: +90 216 465 55 15 Fax: +90 216 465 55 14
Web: www.abkakristal.com, e-mail: altan@abkakristal.com

AEB HOTEL EQUIPMENT INC.
Tel: +90 242 322 90 56 Fax: +90 242 322 60 50
Web: www.aebhotelequipments.com,
e-mail: info@aebhotelequipments.com

AHMETAL
Tel: +90 272 612 88 02 Gsm: 009 0532 451 60 82
Web: www.ahmetal.com.tr, e-mail: export@ahmetal.com.tr

AKAY PLASTIC INDUSTRY TRADE INC.
Tel: +90 212 659 11 87 Fax: +90 212 659 11 89
Web: www.akayplastik.com.tr, e-mail: info@akayplastik.com.tr

AKCAM GLASS PLASTIC CONSTRUCTION CO.
Tel: +90 216 378 74 50 Fax: +90 216 378 87 30
Web: www.ak-cam.com.tr, e-mail: export@ak-cam.com.tr

AKDEM MUTFAK GEREÇLERİ ÇELİK SAN. TİC. LTD.ŞTİ
Tel: +90 344 236 34 01 Fax: +90 344 236 34 06
Web: www.akdem.com.tr, e-mail: akdem@akdem.com.tr

AKER ELEKTRİKLİ EV ALETLERİ
Tel: +90 212 876 93 77 Fax: +90 212 876 93 55
Web: www.aker-mutfak.com, e-mail: aker@akerticaret.com

AKSEL KITCHENWARE IND. AND. TRADE
Tel: +90 212 617 12 60 Fax: +90 212 538 22 28
Web: www.akselmutfak.com, e-mail: info@akselmutfak.com.tr

AKYILDIZ MUTFAK EŞYALARI
Tel: +90 344 257 91 88 Fax: +90 344 257 91 87
Web: www.akykitchen.com, e-mail: info@akykitchen.com

AKYOL PLASTİK
Tel: +90 212 550 30 21 Fax: +90 212 550 54 47
Web: www.akyol.com.tr, e-mail: info@akyol.com.tr

AKYÜZ PLASTIC
Tel: +90 212 612 94 00 Fax: +90 212 577 60 92
Web: www.akyuz.com.tr, e-mail: info@akyuz.com.tr

ALBA TURİSTİK VE HEDİYELİK EŞYA
Tel: +90 212 578 87 96 Fax: +90 212 578 87 96
Web: www.albasis.com, e-mail: info@albasis.com

AL-CO ALÜMİNYUM / Papilla
Tel: +90 212 676 78 38 Fax: +90 212 676 78 39
Web: www.alcocookware.com, , www.papilla.com.tr
e-mail: adalgic@alcocookware.com, info@papilla.com.tr

ALBAYRAK MELAMİN PLASTİK
Tel: +90 212 659 33 75 Fax: +90 212 659 33 80
Web: www.albayrakmelamin.com, e-mail: info@albayrakmelamin.com

ALEVLİ ZÜCCACİYE TİCARET A.Ş
Tel: +90 212 219 51 11 Fax: +90 212 225 02 93
Web: www.alevli.com.tr, e-mail: info@alevli.com.tr

ALKAN ZÜCCACİYE SAN. VE TİC. LTD. ŞTİ.
Tel: +90 212 527 15 92 Fax: +90 212 528 13 69
Web: www.alkanzuccaciye.com, e-mail: zicco@alkanzuccaciye.com

ALP PLASTİK KALIP SANAYİ / Moonstar
Tel: +90 212 875 26 66 Fax: +90 212 875 26 46
Web: www.moonstar.com.tr, e-mail: moonstar@moonstar.com.tr

ALPİN STEEL
Tel: +90 212 875 02 22 Fax: +90 212 875 02 26
Web: www.bertone.com.tr, e-mail: info@bertone.com.tr

ALYANS METAL
Tel: +90 344 236 11 65 Fax: +90 344 236 44 25
Web: www.alyansmetal.com.tr, e-mail: info@alyansmetal.com.tr

ANİKYA İZNİK TILE
Tel: +90 216 422 88 41 Fax: +90 216 422 88 43
Web: www.anikya.com, e-mail: info@anikya.com

ANİVA EV URUNLERİ METAL SAN. TİC. LTD. ŞTİ.
Tel: +90 262 751 21 94 Fax: +90 262 751 21 98
Web: www.ayhanmetal.com.tr
e-mail: ayhanmetal@ayhanmetal.com.tr

ANSAN METAL AND PLASTIC
Tel: +90 212 422 05 06 Fax: +90 212 422 85 82
Web: www.ansan.com.tr, e-mail: exp1@ansan.com.tr

ARAS METAL
Tel: +90 212 855 27 80 Fax: +90 212 856 08 26
Web: www.arasmetal.com, e-mail: arasmetal@superonline.com

ARÇELİK
Tel: +90 212 314 34 34 Web: www.arcelik.com.tr
e-mail: melis.mutus@arcelik.com.tr, seher.turkpence@arcelik.com.tr

ARDA GLASSWARE
Tel: +90 212 422 10 66 Fax: +90 212 422 10 71
Web: www.ardaglassware.com
e-mail: contact@ardaglassware.com

ARMA METAL DIS TİC.LTD.ŞTİ.
Tel: +90 344 251 33 00 - Fax: +90 344 251 31 31
Web: www.armametal.com, e-mail: info@armametal.com

ARMADA METAL SANAYİ VE TİCARET LTD. ŞTİ.
Tel: +90 212 694 58 82 - Fax: 212 591 75 54
Web:www.armadametal.com,
e-mail: satis@armadametal.com

ARMONİ A.Ş.
Tel: +90 212 798 36 37 Fax: +90 212 798 36 46
Web: www.armonipazarlama.com, e-mail: armoni@armonipazarlama.com

ARTAÇ KITCHENWARE MANUFACTURING COMPANY
Tel: +90 212 798 25 75 Fax: +90 212 798 25 79
Web: www.artac.com.tr, e-mail: info@artac.com.tr

ACTFILE

ARTEK ELEKTRİKLİ EV ALETLERİ SAN. VE TİC. LTD. ŞTİ.
Tel: +90 212 256 47 63-64 Fax: +90 212 255 04 90
Web: www.ar-tek.com, e-mail: ar-tek@ar-tek.com

ARTEPELLE HEDİYELİK EŞYA
Tel: +90 212 283 29 30 Fax: +90 212 283 29 21
Web: www.arte-pelle.com, e-mail: info@arte-pelle.com

AR-YILDIZ MADENİ MUTFAK EŞYALARI SAN. TİC. A.Ş.
Tel: +90 282 681 84 60 Fax: +90 282 681 84 70
Web: www.aryildiz.com, e-mail: info@aryildiz.com

ARZU ÇELİK METAL SAN. TİC. LTD. ŞTİ. / Asstarline
Tel: +90 344 236 05 03 Fax: +90 344 236 11 87
Web: www.arzumetal.com.tr, e-mail: export@arzumetal.com

ARZUM SMALL DOMESTIC APPLIANCE / Felix
Tel: +90 212 467 80 80 Fax: +90 212 467 80 00
Web: www.arzum.com.tr, www.felix.com.tr
e-mail: okarahan@arzum.com.tr

AS PLASTIC AND PACKAGING
Tel: +90 216 464 38 48 Fax: +90 216 445 79 02
Web: www.asplastik.com, e-mail: export@asplastik.com

A-SİL KABLO SAN.TİC.VE LTD.ŞTİ
Tel: +90 212 486 02 01 Fax: +90 212 485 00 80
Web: www.casta-sil.com, e-mail: info@casta-sil.com

ASİL TİCARET VE EV ALETLERİ / Noble Life
Tel: +90 212 659 51 00 Fax: +90 212 659 25 15
Web: www.asilticaret.com.tr, www.noblelife.com.tr
e-mail: asil@asilticaret.com.tr

ASKOM OTEL RESTAURANT EQUIPMENTS
Tel: +90 212 513 29 38 Fax: +90 212 526 58 94
Web: www.askom.com, e-mail: askom@askom.com

ASUDE PLASTİK KALIP SAN.TİC
Tel: +90 212 659 23 12-13 Fax: +90 212 659 23 11
Web: www.asudeplastik.com, e-mail: muhase@asudeplastik.com

ATA DÖKÜM SAN. VE TİC. A.Ş
Tel: +90 222 236 82 26 Fax: +90 222 236 82 31
Web: www.surelgrup.com, www.atadokum.com.tr; www.surelmutfak.com
e-mail: atadokum@atadokum.com.tr

ATLANTİK TÜKETİM MAL.SAN.TİC.LTD.ŞTİ.
Tel: +90 212 494 47 74 Fax: +90 212 494 47 75
Web: www.dose.com.tr, e-mail: pazarlama@dose.com.tr

ATLAS DAYANIKLI TÜKETİM MALLARI
Tel: +90 212 585 34 44 Fax: +90 212 589 16 25
Web: www.atlasdtm.com, e-mail: atlas@atlasdtm.com

ATMACA ELEKTRONİK / Cleaner, Sunny, Woon, Cendix, Axen
Tel: +90 212 412 12 12 Fax: +90 212 412 14 99
Web: www.sunny.com.tr, e-mail: halilorenbas@sunny.com.tr

AVA PLASTİK SANAYİ / Avatherm
Tel: +90 282 747 63 33 Fax: +90 282 747 65 31
Web: www.avaplastik.com, e-mail: avaplastik@avaplastik.com

AVŞAR ENAMEL SAN. TİC. A.Ş. / Avsar, Rataly
Tel: +90 272 612 66 00 Fax: +90 272 611 43 34
Web: www.avsar.com, e-mail: export@avsar.com
export3@avsar.com

AYDIN TURİSTİK HEDİYELİK EŞYA VE DEKORASYON
Tel: +90 212 512 60 63 Fax: +90 212 513 45 16
Web: www.exoticlamp.com.tr,
e-mail: exoptic@exoticlamp.com.tr

AYKASA POLİMER AMBALAJ VE TAŞIMA SİSTEMLERİ SAN. TİC. A.Ş.
Tel: 0262 653 16 74
www.aykasa.com.tr,info@aykasa.com.tr

AYSBERG SOĞUTMA METAL SAN. VE TİC.A.Ş
Tel: +90212 886 78 00 Fax: +90 212 886 64 83
Web: www.oztiryakiler.com.tr, e-mail: aysberg@oztiryakiler.com.tr

AYMAK ENDÜSTRİYEL MUTFAK CİHAZLARI SAN. VE TİC.A.Ş.
Tel: +90 242 258 17 10 Fax: +90 242 258 17 14
Web: www.oztiryakiler.com.tr, e-mail: aymak@oztiryakiler.com.tr

AYPAS ELEKTRONİK SAN. TİC. A.Ş. / Galaxy
Tel: +90 212 659 93 33 Fax: +90 212 659 93 34
Web: www.aypas.com.tr
e-mail: gyorur@aypas.com.tr, galaxy@aypas.com.tr

AYYILDIZ MUTFAK EŞYALARI TEKSTİL SAN. VE DIŞ TİC. LTD. ŞTİ.
e-mail: info@ayyildizexport.com, Tel: +90 344 231 49 49
Fax:+90 344 231 49 49, www.ayyildizexport.com

BAGER PLASTİK SAN.VE TİCARET LTD.ŞTİ.
Tel: +90 212 659 57 30 Fax: +90 212 659 02 75
Web: www.bagerplastik.com
e-mail: info@bagerplastik.com

BANAT FIRÇA VE PLASTİK SANAYİ
Tel: +90 212 289 01 50 Fax: +90 212 289 08 29
Web: www.banat.com, e-mail: satis@banat.com

BAŞAK MAKİNA MUTFAK EŞYALARI
Tel: +90 212 485 24 73 Fax: +90 212 485 24 77
Web: www.basakmakina.com.tr
e-mail: info@basakmakina.com.tr

BAYİNER ELEKTRONİK
Tel: +90 216 415 53 36 Fax: +90 216 415 27 37
Web: www.bayiner.com.tr, e-mail: info@bayiner.com.tr

BAYRAKTAR MADENİ EŞYA SAN. VE TİC. LTD. ŞTİ.
Tel: +90 212 659 78 00 Fax: +90 212 659 78 02
Web: www.bayraktarkitchenware.com
e-mail: istoc@bayraktarkitchenware.com

BAYSAN HEATING AND COOLING SYSTEMS
Tel: +90 212 501 84 83 Fax: +90 212 576 33 81
Web: www.baysanmutfak.com
e-mail: baysan@baysanmutfak.com

BEKO
Tel: +90 212 314 34 34 Fax: +90 212 314 34 50
Web: www.beko.com.tr, e-mail: melis.mutus@arcelik.com.tr

HOUSEWARE • GIFTWARE • TABLEWARE • INDUSTRIAL • ELECTRICAL • PLASTICWARE • KITCHENWARE

HOUSEWARE • GIFTWARE • TABLEWARE • INDUSTRIAL • ELECTRICAL • PLASTICWARE • KITCHENWARE

BELIVA INTERNATIONAL
Tel: +90 212 659 80 55 Fax: +90 212 659 80 56
Web: www.akelevaletleri.com, e-mail: info@akelevaletleri.com

BEMSA METAL EŞYA SAN. VE TİC.
Tel: +90 344 236 08 84
Web: www.bemsametal.com, e-mail: info@bemsametal.com

BES METAL EŞYA TURİZM KİMYA SAN. TİC. LTD.ŞTİ.
Tel: +90 262 751 48 69 Fax: +90 262 751 48 22
Web: www.besmetal.com, e-mail: info@besmetal.com

BES PLASTİK SANAYİ
Tel: +90 212 876 36 32 Fax: +90 212 876 36 34
Web: www.besplastik.com, e-mail: info@besplastik.com

BEŞTEPE TUBE PROFILE TRADE CO.
Tel: +90 352 322 04 37 Fax: +90 352 322 04 42
Web: www.bestepe.com.tr, e-mail: info@bestepe.com.tr

BİLAL MUTFAK EŞY. SANAYİ VE TİCARET LTD.ŞTİ.
Tel: +90 422 237 55 33 Fax: +90 422 237 55 31
Web: www.bilal.com.tr
e-mail: info@bilal.com.tr

BİLGE METALSAN ÇELİK VE METAL
Tel: +90 212 612 26 30 Fax: +90 212 612 69 12
Web: www.bilgemetal.com
e-mail: bilgemetal@bilgemetal.com

BKL MAKİNE SANAYİ ve TİCARET LTD.ŞTİ
Tel: +90 212 690 37 20-21
Fax: +90 212 428 39 45
Web: www.bklmakine.com
e-mail: bklmakine@bklmakine.com

BLANCO ÖZTİRYAKİLER MUTFAK DONANIMI SAN.
Tel: +90 212 886 57 13 Fax: +90 212 886 57 21
Web: www.blanco.com.tr
e-mail: nadirerbil@blanco.com.tr

BLUE HOUSE-TARMAN DIŞ TİCARET A.Ş.
Tel: +90 212 365 44 44 Pbx Fax: +90 212 365 44 55
Web: www.blue-house.com.tr, e-mail: info@tarmangroup.com

BOĞAZİÇİ INDUSTRIAL
Tel: +90 212 294 22 15 Fax: +90 212 294 97 18
Web: www.bogazicimakina.com, e-mail: bogazici@bogazicimakina.com

BORA PLASTİK SAN. VE TİC. A.Ş.
Tel: +90 212 422 18 50 Fax: +90 212 422 44 34
Web: www.boraplastik.com.tr, e-mail: info@boraplastik.com.tr

BOSCH AND SIEMENS HOME APPLIANCES GROUP
Tel: +90 282 748 30 00 Fax: + 90 282 726 53 96
Web: www.bosch-home.com, e-mail: kurumsaliletisim@bshg.com

BOZTEPE - MEGA STAINLESS STEEL
Tel: +90 258 251 69 90 Fax: +90 258 251 66 10
Web: www.boztepe.com, e-mail: info@boztepe.com

BURÇAK PLASTIC COMPANY
Tel: +90 212 674 75 75 Fax: +90 212 577 77 95
Web: www.burcakplast.com.tr
e-mail: info@burcakplast.com.tr

BURSEV PLASTIC&FOREIGN TRADE
Tel: +90 212 659 06 91 Fax: +90 212 659 06 97
Web: www.bursev.com, e-mail: info@bursev.com

BUTANSAN HOMEWARE
Tel: +90 352 322 00 90 Fax: +90 352 322 00 99
Web: www.butansan.com.tr, e-mail: butansan@hotmail.com.tr

CAMBRO ÖZAY PLASTİK / Ozay, Cambro
Tel: +90 262 751 29 40 Fax: +90 262 751 18 79
Web: www.ozaytray.com, e-mail: ozaytray@ozaytray.com

CAN CAN JUICERS AND KITCHEN EQUIPMENTS
Tel: +90 264 291 49 44 Fax: +90 264 291 49 45
Web: www.cancan.com.tr, www.cancanmakina.com.tr
e-mail: info@cancanmakina.com

CANBA
Tel: +90 212 325 94 13 Fax: +90 212 325 94 12
Web: www.canba.com.tr, e-mail: info@canba.com.tr

CAPRI INDUSTRIAL COOLING & KITCHEN
Tel: +90 224 484 31 15 Fax: +90 224 484 31 17
Web: www.capri.com.tr, e-mail: capri@capri.com.tr

CEM BİALETTİ EV VE MUTFAK EŞYALARI / Cem
Tel: +90 216 445 53 73 Fax: +90 216 445 53 74
Web: www.cembialetti.com
e-mail: info@cembialetti.com

CEMİLE DIŞ TİC. LTD.ŞTİ.
Tel: +90 212 249 91 34 - +90 212 251 58 16
Fax: +90 212 249 91 76
Web: www.cemile.com.tr, e-mail: cemile@cemile.com.tr

CENK METAL - ZEST COOKWARES
Tel: +90 212 567 24 56 Fax: +90 212 544 59 39
Web: www.cenkmetal.com
e-mail: info@cenkmetal.com

ÇELİKAY INDUSTRIAL
Tel: +90 312 319 08 09 Fax: +90 312 319 20 60
Web: www.celikay.com.tr, e-mail: celikay@celikay.com.tr

ÇETİN PLASTİK KALIP SAN.VE TİC.LTD.ŞTİ.
Tel: +90 212 537 48 48 fax: +90 212 537 30 29
Web:www.cetinplastik.com.tr
e-mail:Office@cetinplastik.com.tr
mdeniz@cetinplastik.com.tr

ÇETİN PLASTİK SAN. TİC.LTD.ŞTİ.
Tel: +90 212 502 21 28
Web:www.cetinplastik.com
e-mail:ugur.ozkan@cetinplastik.com

ÇETİNTAŞ BEYAZ EŞYA
Tel: +90 222 236 00 55 Fax: +90 222 235 05 75
Web: www.cetintasbeyazesya.com
e-mail: export@cetintasbeyazesya.com

ÇÖZÜM MUTFAK SAN. VE TİC. A.Ş.
Tel: +90 232 376 72 76 Fax: +90 232 376 72 78
Web: www.cozummutfak.com, e-mail: izmirsts@cozummutfak.com

DALGIÇ GÜMÜŞ SAN. VE DIŞ TİC. LTD. ŞTİ.
Tel: +90 212 482 42 00 Fax: +90 212 482 42 18
Web: www.dalgic.com.tr, e-mail: dalgic@dalgic.com.tr

DAY-CO METAL
Tel: +90 212 493 51 62 Fax: +90 212 493 51 38
Web: www.day-cometal.com, e-mail: info@day-cometal.com

DECORIUM/AR-ŞAH KRİSTAL
Tel: +90 216 595 18 63 Fax: +90 216 378 53 51
Web: www.decorium.com.tr
e-mail: info@decorium.com.tr

DEKOR AHŞAP ÜRÜNLERİ SAN. A.Ş.
Tel: +90 262 678 65 00 Fax: +90 262 642 56 85
Web: www.lineadecor.com.tr
e-mail: export@lineadecor.com.tr,
nazan.kartal@lineadecor.com.tr

DEKOR GLASSWARE FOREIGN TRADE CO.
Tel: +90 212 422 17 01 Fax: +90 212 422 79 73
Web: www.dekorcam.com.tr, e-mail: export@dekorcam.com.tr

DEMİREL PLASTİK VE KALIP SANAYİ
Tel: +90 212 659 59 21 Fax: + 90 212 659 59 23
Web: www.demirelplastik.com, Web: export@demirelplastik.com

DENGE GIDA ÜRÜNLERİ ELEKTRİK ELEK. DAN. VE PAZ.
Tel: +90 212 576 82 81 Fax: +90 212 577 71 17
Web: www.denge-ltd.com.tr, e-mail: info@denge-ltd.com.tr

DENİZLİ CAM SAN. VE TİC. A.Ş.
Tel: +90 212 377 27 65 Fax: +90 212 350 42 73
Web: www.denizlicam.com.tr

DERİA DERİ SANAYİ
Tel: +90 216 573 46 58 Fax: +90 216 573 46 58
Web: www.deria.com.tr, e-mail: ugur@deria.com.tr

DESİNG ZONE GALLERY
Tel: +90 212 527 92 85
Web:www.ozlemtuna.com, e-mail:info@ozlemtuna.com

DİBEKSAN MET. MAT. İHR. İTH. SAN. TİC. LTD. ŞTİ.
Tel: +90 236 313 65 10 Fax: +90 236 314 20 98
Web: www.dibeksan.com, e-mail: dibeksan@dibeksan.com

DİKTAŞ INC. CO.
Tel: +90 312 267 01 90 Fax: +90 312 267 10 03 Web: www.diktas.com,
e-mail: diktas@diktas.com, export1@diktas.com

DİZDAR STAINLESS STEEL KITCHEN EQUIPMENT CO.
Tel: +90 212 444 20 98 Fax: +90 212 690 12 57
Web: www.dizdarsteel.com, e-mail: info@dizdarsteel.com

DKR-DEKOR BANYO
Tel: +90 216 466 56 83 Fax: +90 216 527 53 82
Web: www.dekorbanyo.com, e-mail: info@dekorbanyo.com

DMR SEDEFÇİLİK
Tel: +0506 547 02 03 - 0539 324 23 76
Web: www.dmrsedefcilik.com.tr, e-mail: mozaiksedefkakma@gmail.com

DOĞRULAR MADENİ EŞYA PAZ. LTD. ŞTİ.
Tel: +90 332 239 16 40 Fax: +90 332 239 16 49
Web: www.dogrular.com.tr, e-mail: emin@dogrular.com.tr
mahir@dogrular.com.tr

DOLPHİN ÇÖKERTME CAM SANAYİ
Tel: +90 216 631 66 32 Fax: +90 216 632 19 32
Web: www.dolphinglass.com.tr, e-mail: info@dolphinglass.com.tr

DÜNYA PLASTİK SAN.
Tel: +90 212 489 04 14 Fax: +90 212 489 16 11
Web: www.dunyaplastik.com, e-mail: export@dunyaplastik.com

ECE METAL SAN. VE TİC. LTD. ŞTİ.
Tel: +90 212 481 83 17 Fax: +90 212 481 82 50
Web: www.ecemetal.com.tr, e-mail: info@ecemetal.com.tr

EFBA DAYANIKLI TÜK. MAL. SAN.
Tel: +90 212 486 38 20 Fax: +90 212 486 38 42
Web: www.efba.com.tr, e-mail: info@efba.com.tr

EFE CAM SAN. İTH. İHR.
Tel: +90 212 479 51 51 Fax: +90 212 477 27 88
Web: www.efecam.com.tr, e-mail: export@efecam.com.tr

EFEM MUTFAK
Tel: +90 212 591 20 22 Fax: +90 212 591 60 22
Web: www.efemmutfak.com, e-mail: info@efemmutfak.com

EFES HEDİYELİK EŞYA SAN.
Tel: +90 212 511 30 37 Fax: +90 212 514 59 40
Web: www.colorlightscollection.com, e-mail: info@mosaiclampstore.com

EGE EV ÜRÜNLERİ MADENİ EŞYA PAZARLAMA SAN. VE TİC. LTD. ŞTİ.
Tel: +90 232 853 73 80 Fax: +90 232 853 70 05
Web: www.egeltd.net, e-mail: info@egeltd.net

EGEMEN HEDİYELİK EŞYA OYUNCAK ZÜCCACİYE ELEK.GIDA TEKSTİL İNŞ. AMBALAJ SAN. A.Ş.
Tel: +90 232 437 32 05 Fax: +90 232 437 30 65
Web: www.magicsaverbag.com, e-mail: info@egemen-group.com

EKBER KITCHEN EQUIPMENTS IND.& TRADE CO.
Tel: +90 212 423 92 92 Fax: +90 212 428 17 58
Web: www.ekber.com, e-mail: export@ ekber.com

HOUSEWARE
GIFTWARE
TABLEWARE
INDUSTRIAL
ELECTRICAL
PLASTICWARE
KITCHENWARE

kitchen
turkish
ware

Sidebar legend (bottom to top):
● KITCHENWARE
● PLASTICWARE
● ELECTRICAL
● INDUSTRIAL
● TABLEWARE
● GIFTWARE
● HOUSEWARE

EKONOMA MUTFAK VE SERVİS EKİPMAN SAN. VE TİC. A.Ş.
Tel: +90 212 886 88 00 - 886 88 00 Fax: +90 212 886 68 17
Web: www.oztiryakiler.com.tr, e-mail: ekonoma@oztiryakiler.com.tr

EKSPOPLAST PLASTIC PACKAGING IND.
Tel: +90 216 304 04 24 Fax: +90 216 304 04 29
Web: www.expoplastplastic.com, e-mail: info@expoplastplastic.com

ELEVSAN ELECTRICAL APPLIANCES IND.
Tel: +90 222 236 00 93 Fax: +90 222 236 00 94
Web: www.esco.com.tr, e-mail: export@esco.com.tr

ELİF PLASTİK MUTFAK EŞYALARI
Tel: +90 212 659 22 56 Fax: +90 212 659 56 07
Web: www.elifplastic.com, e-mail: info@elifplastic.com

ELİT FOREIGN TRADE LTD. CO.
Tel: +90 236 237 93 91 Fax: +90 236 238 96 58
Web: www.elitforeigntrade.com, e-mail: info@elitforeigntrade.com
export@elitforeigntrade.com

EMSAN MUTFAK GEREÇLERİ SANAYİ VE TİCARET A.Ş.
Tel: +90 212 495 22 22 Fax: + 90 212 495 45 00
Web: www.emsan.com.tr, Web: info@emsan.com.tr

ENART ENAMEL CO.
Tel: +90 352 321 35 51 Fax: +90 352 321 35 54
Web: www.enartco.com, e-mail: export@enartco.com

ENESCO
Tel: +90 212 520 34 86 Fax: +90 212 520 34 88
Web: www.enescoglass.com, e-mail: info@enescoglass.com

ENKAY ALÜMİNYUM LEVHA MUTFAK EŞYALARI
Tel: +90 362 266 76 26 Fax: +90 362 266 76 27
Web: www.leydimutfak.com, e-mail: leydi@leydimutfak.com

ERA HOME APPLIANCES
Tel: +90 212 407 01 15 – 16 Fax: +90 212 407 01 14
Web: www.eraizgara.com, e-mail: era@eraizgara.com

ERDAL INDUSTRIAL KITCHEN EQUIPMENT
Tel: +90 332 251 51 15 Fax: +90 332 251 51 75
Web: www.erdalmutfak.com.tr,
e-mail: bilgi@erdalmutfak.com.tr

ERDEM KITCHENWARE INDUSTRY
Tel: +90 212 683 22 46 Fax: +90 212 683 22 29
Web: www.erdemkitchen.com, e-mail: ifergan@erdemkitchen.com,
erdem@erdemkitchen.com

ERKOÇ PLASTİK VE KALIP SAN. VE TİC. LTD. ŞTİ.
Tel: +90 212 549 53 85 Fax: +90 212 549 53 87
Web: www.poly-time.com, e-mail: erkoc@poly-time.com

ERNA MAŞ MAKİNA TİC. VE SAN. A.Ş
Tel: +90 212 866 22 00 Fax: +90 212 771 45 00
Web: www.ernamas.com, e-mail: emreg@ernamas.com

ESCO EMAYE DÖKÜM SAN. VE TİC. A.Ş.
Tel: +90 222 236 00 93 Fax: +90 222 236 14 01
Web: www.esco.com.tr, e-mail: export@esco.com.tr

ES-MAK MAKİNE İMALAT SAN.
Tel: +90 212 875 78 16 Fax: +90 212 876 15 33
Web: www.esmak.com.tr, e-mail: mail@esmak.com.tr

ESLON MUTFAK EŞYALARI SAN.VE TİC.LTD.ŞTİ.
Tel: +90 344 257 93 30 Fax: +90 344 257 93 76
Web: www.eslon.com.tr, e-mail: info@eslon.com.tr

ESMER HEDİYELİK
Tel: +90 212 513 76 98 Fax: +90 212 512 17 87
Web: www.esmerbujiteri.com
e-mail: esmer@esmerbujiteri.com

EURO-MEL
Tel: +90 212 486 23 01 Fax: +90 212 486 23 25
Web: www.euro-mel.com,
e-mail: ugur@euro-mel.com, onur@euro-mel.com

EVAS EV ALETLERİ SANAYİ LTD. ŞTİ.
Tel: +90 216 378 73 15 PBX Fax: + 90 216 378 10 06
Web: www.evas.com.tr, e-mail: info@evas.com.tr

EVELİN
Tel: +90 212 659 03 86 Fax: + 90 212 659 03 80
Web: www.evelin.com.tr, e-mail: info@evelin.com.tr

EVREN MUTFAK EŞYALARI SAN.
Tel: +90 212 624 52 21 Fax: +90 212 540 05 00
Web: www.evrenmutfak.com.tr
e-mail: info@evrenmutfak.com.tr

EVREN PLASTİK VE MELAMİN SAN.
Tel: +90 212 550 46 55 Fax: +90 212 550 18 12
Web: www.evrenplastik.com.tr, e-mail: info@evrenplastik.com.tr

EVYELÜKS METAL SAN. TİC. A.Ş.
Tel: +90 212 723 69 00 Fax: +90 212 723 69 19
Web: www.artenova.com.tr, e-mail: info@artenova.com.tr

FAGOR ENDÜSTRİYEL SAN.
Tel: +90 262 751 10 31 Fax: +90 262 751 10 32
Web: www.fagor.com.tr, e-mail: fagor@fagor.com.tr

FATİH PLASTİK SAN.
Tel: +90 352 321 40 70
Web: www.fatihplastik.com, e-mail: info@fatihplastik.com

FETTAH ÇİNİ GIDA TEKSTİL TURİZM SAN. VE TİC. LTD. ŞTİ.
Tel: +90 274 266 22 02 Fax: +90 274 266 26 36
e-mail: fettahceramic@hotmail.com

FİL GRUP - FİLPA
Tel: +90 212 886 32 41 Fax: +90 212 886 32 64
Web: www.filgrup.com.tr, e-mail: info@filgrup.com.tr

FLORKİM
Tel: +90 216 466 82 72 pbx Fax: +90 216 365 23 05
Web: www.florkim.com, -mail: florkim@florkim.com

FORM KITCHEN APPLIANCES
Tel: +90 236 671 38 83 Fax: +90 212 671 38 84
Web: www.form-co.com, e-mail: form.co@form-co.com

FORM PLASTİK SAN. VE TİC. LTD. ŞTİ.
Tel: +90 236 214 01 13 Fax: +90 236 214 01 17
Web: www.formplastik.com.tr, e-mail: info@formplastik.com.tr

FRENOKS ENDÜSTRİYEL SOĞUTMA SANAYİ
Tel: +90 212 544 98 83 Fax: +90 212 493 42 11
Web: www.frenox.com, e-mail: info@frenox.com, burak@frenox.com

FRL FREELINE INDUSTRIAL CLEANING EQUIPMENTS
Tel: +90 212 674 75 75 Fax: +90 212 577 77 95
Web: www.freeline.com, e-mail: info@burcakplast.com.tr

GASTRODİZAYN INDUSTRIAL KITCHEN IND.
Tel: +90 212 297 11 00 Fax: +90 212 254 11 55
Web: www.gastrodizayn.com.tr, e-mail: gastrodizayn@gastrodizayn.com.tr

GD CRYSTAL
Tel: +90 212 613 74 47 Fax: +90 212 576 80 55
Web: www.gundogdukristal.com, e-mail: oktay@gundogdukristal.com

GLANGE CANDLES
Tel: +90 216 420 49 51 Fax: + 90 216 420 15 80
Web: www.glange.org, e-mail: info@glange.org

GLOBAL FOREIGN TRADE LTD. CO.
Tel: +90 258 211 83 57 Fax: +90 258 211 02 62
Web: www.globalcookware.com, e-mail: info@globalcookware.com

GLORE GLASSWARE - SAHRA CAM SAN.
Tel: +90 262 751 18 88 Fax: +90 262 751 18 69
Web: www.gloreglass.com, e-mail: info@gloreglass.com

GOLDEN FLORA
Tel: +90 216 328 64 27 Fax: +90 216 335 77 99
Web: www.goldenflora.com, e-mail: info@goldenflora .com

GOLDİNİ KRİSTAL
Tel: +90 216 320 51 41 Fax: +90 216 320 42 23
Web: www.goldini.com.tr, e-mail: info@goldini.com.tr

GONDOL PLASTIC INDUSTRY
Tel: +90 212 659 90 90 Fax: +90 212 659 87 77
Web: www.gondolplastic.com, e-mail: info@gondolplastic.com

GÖNEN METAL INDUSTRY
Tel: +90 212 552 25 08 Fax: +90 212 551 02 81
Web: www.biricik.com.tr, e-mail: biricik@biricik.com.tr

GÖRGEL METAL SAN. TİC. A.Ş.
Tel: +90 344 236 26 37 Fax: +90 344 236 30 90
Web: www.gorgelmetal.com.tr, e-mail: info@gorgelmetal.com.tr

GRAF IMPORT EXPORT AND TOURISM LTD. CO.
Tel: +90 212 482 02 25 Fax: +90 212 481 97 37
Web: www.graf.com.tr, e-mail: info@graf.com.tr

GRANİT DAYANIKLI TÜKETİM MALLARI
Tel: +90 232 853 91 00 Fax: +90 232 853 85 86
Web: www.granitltdsti.com.tr, e-mail: info@granitltdsti.com.tr

GUESTINHOUSE
Tel: +90 216 385 55 11 Fax: +90 216 385 55 13
Web: www.guestinhouse.com, e-mail: info@guestinhouse.com

GÜLİSTAN DEKAL ÇIKARTMA VE BASKI SAN.
Tel: +90 216 311 46 36 Fax: +90 216 311 36 50
Web: www.gulistandekal.com.tr, e-mail: gd@gulistandekal.com.tr

GÜNEŞ ENAMEL IND AND TRADE CO.
Tel: +90 212 512 95 69 Fax: + 90 212 520 02 60
Web: www.gunesmelamin.com, e-mail: ersan@gunesmelamin.com

GÜNEYSİ METAL MUTFAK EŞYALARI SAN.VE TİC.LTD.ŞTİ.
Tel: +90 344 236 00 15 Fax: +90 344 236 00 14
Web: www.guneysimetal.com.tr, e-mail: mehmet@guneysimetal.com.tr

GÜRÇELİK DAY. TÜK. MAM.
Tel: +90 232 853 92 00 Fax: +90 232 853 91 99
Web: www.gurcelik.com.tr, e-mail: gurcelik@gurcelik.com.tr

GÜREN METAL
Tel: +90 212 549 45 40 Fax: +90 212 549 45 39
Web: www.guren.com.tr, e-mail: info@guren.com.tr

GÜLBAK BAKALİT VE METAL SANAYİ TİCARET LTD. ŞTİ.
Tel: +90 344 236 46 26 Fax: +90 344 236 18 39
Web: www.gulbak.com.tr, e-mail: info@gulbak.com.tr

GÜNEŞ PLASTİK
Tel: +90 262 751 30 16 Fax: +90 262 751 25 00
Web: www.gunesplastik.com.tr, e-mail: info@gunesplastik.com.tr

GÜRAL PORCELAIN HERİŞ CERAMIC
Tel: +90 274 225 03 00 Fax: +90 274 225 03 16
Web: www.guralporselen.com.tr,
e-mail: export@guralporselen.com.tr

GÜRALLAR ARTCRAFT
Tel: +90 216 576 25 25 +90 216 576 25 00
Web: www.artcraft.com.tr
e-mail: artcraft@artcraft.com.tr

GÜR-PAK MELAMİN VE PLAST. SAN. VE TİC.LTD.ŞTİ
Tel: +90 212 486 23 01-02 Fax: +90 212 486 23 25
Web: www.euro-mel.com
e-mail: info@euro-mel.com, onur@euro-mel.com

GÜZELEV - MIACASA
Tel: +90 232 479 12 12 Fax: +90 232 479 92 48
Web: www.guzelev.com.tr, e-mail: info@guzelev.com.tr

● HOUSEWARE
● GIFTWARE
● TABLEWARE
● INDUSTRIAL
● ELECTRICAL
● PLASTICWARE
● KITCHENWARE

HOUSEWARE
GIFTWARE
TABLEWARE
INDUSTRIAL
ELECTRICAL
PLASTICWARE
KITCHENWARE

GÜZELİŞ PORSELEN SAN. TİC. A.Ş. / Eternity
Tel: +90 216 598 35 35 Fax: +90 216 598 35 25
Web: www.guzelis.com.tr, e-mail: info@guzelis.com.tr

HAK PLASTİK AMBALAJ SAN.
Tel: +90 322 441 10 44 Fax: +90 322 441 02 44
Web: www.hakplastik.com.tr, e-mail: hakplastik@hakplastik.com.tr

HAKART DEKORATİF EŞYA VE METAL SAN. ve TİC. A.Ş.
Tel: +90 212 876 26 86 Fax: +90 212 876 26 88
Web: www.hakart.com.tr, e-mail: hakart@hakart.com.tr

HAMAM KONFEKSİYON PAZ.TEKS. SAN. TİC. LTD.ŞTİ.
Tel: +90 258 269 15 56 Fax: +90 258 269 15 59
Web: www.hamam.eu, e-mail: info@hamam.eu

HASCEVHER METAL SAN. / Hascevher, Hcm, Arian, Perfect
Tel: +90 344 257 95 70 Fax: +90 344 257 95 64
Web: www.hascevher.com.tr, e-mail: info@hascevher.com.tr

HAY FIRÇA SAN.
Tel: +90 232 264 60 17 Fax: + 90 232 264 76 10
Web: www.hayfirca.com, e-mail: info@hayfirca.com

HECHA CAST IRON COOKWARE FOR GOURMETS
Tel: +90 212 445 10 20 Fax: +90 212 445 79 79
Web: www.hecha.com.tr, e-mail: info@hecha.com.tr

HELENA SEDEFLİ MOBİLYA LTD. ŞTİ.
Tel: +90 326 285 62 08 Fax: +90 326 285 62 10
Web: www.helena.com.tr, e-mail: helena@helena.com.tr

**HEREVIN SOLMAZER KITCHENWARE INDUSTRY
LTD / Herevin, Mayamos**
Tel: +90 212 659 00 19 Fax: +90 212 659 40 46
Web: www.solmazer.com, e-mail: info@solmazer.com
export@solmazer.com

Hİ-PAŞ PLASTİK EŞYA TİC.VE SAN.LTD.ŞTİ.
Tel: +90 212 659 03 86 Fax: +90 212 659 03 80
Web: www.evelin.com.tr, www.hipas.com.tr
e-mail: info@evelin.com.tr; info@hipas.com.tr

HİREF TASARIM ORG. VE DIŞ TİC.
Tel: +90 212 283 15 77 Fax: +90 212 283 15 78
Web: www.hiref.com.tr, e-mail: info@hirefstore.com.tr

HİSAR CUTLERY AND COOKWARE PRODUCT
Tel: +90 212 596 10 03 Fax: +90 212 596 10 35
Web: www.hisar.com.tr, e-mail: export@hisar.com.tr

HOMATEX TURİZM VE OTEL MALZ.
Tel: +90 212 320 32 55 Fax: +90 212 320 32 50
Web: www.homatex.com.tr, e-mail: homatex@homatex.com.tr

HOTEC TOURISM IND IMPORT EXPORT
Tel: +90 212 320 30 70 Fax: +90 212 221 33 74
Web: www.hotecturkey.com, e-mail: esene@hotecturkey.com

HÜRSULTAN CO.
Tel: +90 212 798 25 60 Fax: +90 212 798 25 69
Web: www.hursultan.com.tr, e-mail: info@hursultan.com.tr

ICF KITCHEN APPLIANCES
Tel: +90 216 575 51 54 Fax: +90 216 572 44 27
Web: www.icfappliances.com, e-mail: cenk@icfappliances.com

ILIO
Tel: +90 212 245 25 63 Fax: +90 212 244 89 43
Web: www.demirden.com, e-mail: info@demirden.com

INDESIT COMPANY
Tel: +90 212 355 53 00 Fax: +90 212 216 13 73
Web: www.hotpoint.com.tr

IRAK PLASTİK SANAYİ
Tel: +90 212 659 54 12 Fax: + 90 212 659 51 08
Web: www.irakplast.com, e-mail: expo@irakplast.com,
pazarlama@irakplast.com, sibel@irakplast.com

ISITAŞ BEYAZ EŞYA SAN. VE TİC. A.Ş.
Tel: +90 222 236 16 63 - 64 Fax: +90 222 236 16 65
Web: www.sunfire.com.tr, e-mail: export@sunfire.com.tr

**IŞILAY MUTFAK EŞYALARI BAKALİT METAL
TEKS.TAŞ.İNŞ.GIDA SAN.TİC.LTD.STİ.**
Tel: +90 344 236 09 64 Fax: +90 344 236 09 75
e-mail: info@isilaymetal.com

İKRA METAL STANLIESS STEEL INDUSTRY
Tel: +90 344 236 40 00 Fax: +90 344 236 40 40
Web: www.ikragroup.com, e-mail: ikratrade@ikragroup.com

İLYASOĞLU EVIL EYES
Tel: +90 212 513 34 49 Fax: +90 212 310 24 95
Web: www.ilyasoglu.com, e-mail: contact@ilyasoglu.com

İNCİ MADENİ EŞYA
Tel: +90 212 597 60 34 Fax: +90 212 597 52 13
Web: www.incicelik.com.tr, e-mail: incicelik@incicelik.com.tr

İNOKSAN A.Ş. / İnoksdesign, Klinoks
Tel: +90 224 294 74 74 Fax: +90 224 243 61 23
Web: www.inoksan.com.tr, e-mail: inoksan@inoksan.com.tr

İPEK ZÜC. IMPORT & EXPORT CO. LTD.
Tel: +90 212 659 24 28 Fax: +90 212 659 55 30
Web: www.ipekltd.com, e-mail: export@carmelia.com.tr

İTİMAT MAKİNA SANAYİ
Tel: +90 352 321 26 26 Fax: +90 352 321 18 03
Web: www.itimat.com.tr, e-mail: itimat@itimat.com.tr

**İZMAK INDUSTRIAL KITCHEN
EQUIPMENTS MANUFACTURER**
Tel: +90 232 281 44 64 Fax: +90 232 281 51 25
Web: www.izmak.com.tr, e-mail: izmak@izmak.com.tr

ACTFILE

JUMBO MADENİ MUTFAK EŞYA SAN.
Tel: +90 212 565 90 70 Fax: +90 212 565 60 47
Web: www.jumbo.com.tr, e-mail: info@jumbo.com.tr

KABOĞLU PLASTIC PACKAGING IND. TRADE
Tel: +90 216 304 04 24 Fax: +90 216 304 02 29
Web: www.kablogluplastik.com, faruk@kablogluplastik.com

KALIPSAN KALIP PLASTİK VE AMBALAJ SAN.
Tel: +90 212 422 92 43 Fax: +90 212 422 68 85
Web: www.kalıpsanplastik.com.tr
e-mail: info@kalipsanplastik.com.tr

KALİTE INDUSTRIAL KITCHEN APPLIANCES IND.
Tel: +90 212 671 99 34 Fax: + 90 212 671 99 44
Web: www.kalitegaz.com.tr, e-mail: info@kalitegaz.com.tr

KAR MAKİNA PARÇALARI SAN. / Omg Innova
Tel: +90 262 751 03 90 Fax: +90 262 751 03 94
Web: www.omginnova.com e-mail: mustafa@omginnova.com

KAR TEKNİK SOĞUTMA ENDÜSTRİYEL MUTFAK SAN.
Tel: +90 242 258 18 50 Fax: +90 242 258 18 55
Web: www.karteknik.com, karteknik@karteknik.com

KARACA ZÜCCACİYE TİC. SAN. A.Ş.
Tel: +90 212 412 44 00 Fax: +90 212 422 48 59
Web: www.krc.com.tr, e-mail: krc@krc.com.tr

KARAKAYA PLASTIC LTD. ŞTİ.
Tel: +90 212 567 23 19 Fax: +90 212 577 06 94
Web: www.karakayaplastik.com, e-mail: karakaya@karakayaplastik.com

KARAT TAKI VE MÜCEVHERAT SAN. TİC. A.Ş.
Tel: +90 232 462 06 06 Fax: +90 232 462 05 05
Web: www.karatgold.com.tr, e-mail: info@karatgold.com.tr

KARDESAN BAKERY AND PASTRY EQUIPMENTS
Tel: +90 216 471 84 61 Fax: +90 216 471 84 62
Web: www.kardesan.com, e-mail: info@kardesan.com

KARTAL INDUSTRIAL KITCHEN APPLIANCES
Tel: +90 212 428 09 04 Fax: +90 212 428 09 07
Web: www.kartalmutfak.com,e-mail: info@kartalmutfak.com

KASTAMONU PLASTİK PACKAGING PRODUCTS
Tel: +90 212 509 32 99 Fax: +90 212 676 39 06
Web: www.kastamonuplastik.com, e-mail: info@kastamonuplastik.com

KAVSAN
Tel: +90 212 552 01 39 Fax: +90 212 522 40 71
Web: www.kavsan.com, e-mail: kavsan@kavsan.com

KAYALAR ENDÜSTRİYEL MUTFAK SANAYİ /
Folnox, Electromax, Mastro
Tel: +90 212 612 26 11 Fax: +90 212 493 10 16
Web: www.kayalarmutfak.com
e-mail: info@kayalarmutfak.com

KAYALAR STEEL CO.
Tel: +90 212 859 00 02 Fax: +90 212 859 00 14
Web: www.kayalar.com.tr, e-mail: kayalar@kayalar.com.tr

KAYALAR MUTFAK-OTEL-RESTAURANT EKİPMANLARI
Tel: +90 232 479 79 90 Fax: + 90 232 479 79 94
Web: www.kayalar.gen.tr
e-mail: osman@kayalar.gen.tr

KERAMİKA SERAMİK
Tel: +90 274 266 20 02 Fax: +90 274 266 24 55
Web: www.keramika.com.tr, e-mail: fyuce@unsamadencilik.com.tr

KILIÇLAR ÇATAL KAŞIK MADENİ MUTFAK EŞYALARI
Tel: +90 216 592 82 00 Fax: +90 216 592 24 55
Web: www.kiliclar.net, e-mail: kiliclar@superonline.com

KING PAZARLAMA VE DIŞ TİC. A.Ş.
Tel: +90 212 565 15 95 Fax: +90 212 565 16 07
Web: www.king.com.tr, e-mail: pazarlama@king.com.tr

KIRTEKSMETAL TEKSTİL SAN. VE TİC. LTD.ŞTİ.
Tel: +90 344 257 91 43 Fax: +90 344 257 91 46
Web: www.kirteksmetal.com, e-mail: info@kirteksmetal.com

KIZIKOĞLU INDUSTRIAL COOLING INDUSTRY
Tel: +90 274 224 93 92 Fax: +90 274 224 93 90
Web: www.sogutmaci.com, e-mail: export@sogutmaci.com

KLASS FOREIGN TRADE LTD. CO.
Tel: +90 352 321 13 79 Fax: +90 352 321 18 43
Web: www.klass.com.tr, e-mail: info@klass.com.tr
export.class@gmail.com

KLEO MINIBAR & ROOM SERVICE EQUIPMENTS
Tel: +90 242 321 46 76 Fax: +90 242 321 47 17
Web: www.minibar.com.tr, e-mail: info@minibar.com.tr

KONYA SARAYLI MADENİ EŞYA / Saraylı
Tel: +90 332 239 08 78 Fax: +90 332 239 02 36
Web: www.smsarayli.com.tr, e-mail: info@smsarayli.com.tr

KORKMAZ STAINLESS STEEL COOKWARE & ELECTRICAL
Tel: +90 216 444 01 47 Fax: +90 216 540 09 34
Web: www.korkmaz.com.tr, e-mail: info@korkmaz.com.tr

KRISTAL INDUSTRIAL
Tel: +90 242 258 03 22 Fax: +90 242 258 00 68
Web: www.kristalendustriyel.com
mail: info@kristalendustriyel.com, u.acar@ kristalendustriyel.com

KROMÇELIK STAINLESS STEEL SINKS
Tel: +90 212 771 53 53 Fax: +90 212 771 53 63
Web: www.kromcelik.com.tr, e-mail: info@kromcelik.com.tr

KROMEVYE SAN. TİC. LTD. ŞTİ.
Tel: +90 212 886 55 88 (pbx) Fax: +90 212 886 57 14
Web: www.kromevye.com.tr, e-mail: info@kromevye.com.tr

HOUSEWARE · GIFTWARE · TABLEWARE · INDUSTRIAL · ELECTRICAL · PLASTICWARE · KITCHENWARE

KROMLÜKS MUTFAK CİHAZLARI
Tel: +90 312 231 84 50 Fax: +90 312 231 45 92
Web: www.kromluks.com, e-mail: kromluks@kromluks.com

KÜÇÜK ESNAF TURİSTİK EŞYA İMALATI
Tel: +90 212 511 23 62 Fax: +90 212 511 23 62
Web: www.artmosaiclamp.com, e-mail: info@artmosaiclamp.com

KÜLSAN ENAMEL PLASTIC
Tel: +90 212 477 56 66 Fax: + 90 212 618 19 70
Web: www.kulsan.com.tr, e-mail: kulsan@kulsan.com.tr

KÜTAHYA PORSELEN SAN. A.Ş.
Tel: +90 274 225 01 50 Fax: +90 274 225 12 08
Web: www.kutahyaporselen.com.tr
e-mail: nmercan@kutahyaporselen.com

LAVA METAL DÖKÜM SAN. TİC. A.Ş.
Tel: +90 216 312 26 53 Fax: +90 216 312 09 09
Web: www.lavametal.com.tr
e-mail: satis@lavametal.com.tr

LEYDİ NON-STICK COOKWARE
Tel: +90 212 659 54 67
Web: www.leydimutfak.com, e-mail: leydi@leydimutfak.com

LSB DIŞ TİC. VE DAN. LTD. ŞTİ.
Tel: +90 216 413 82 53 Fax: +90 216 425 46 59
Web: www.lsbgroup.com
e-mail: info@lsbgroup.com, mesutbudak@lsbgroup.com

LUX PLASTIC / Avantage, Bosfor, Seher, Avantaj Ev
Tel: +90 212 659 11 26 Fax: +90 212 659 25 46
Web: www.luxplastic.com, e-mail: info@luxplastic.com

LUYANO ZÜCCACİYE TEKSTİL SAN. VE TİC. LTD. ŞTİ.
Tel: +90 212 292 31 63 Fax: +90 212 292 31 49
Web: www.luyano.com.tr, e-mail: info@luyano.com.tr

MAIN STEEL TRADE LTD. CO.
Tel: +90 212 875 42 00 Fax: +90 212 875 42 09
Web: www.maintuna.com, e-mail: info@maintuna.com

MAKPA A.Ş.
Tel: +90 212 256 83 50 Fax: +90 212 250 40 53
Web: www.makpa.com, e-mail: istmakpa@makpa.com

MAKSAN MUTFAK SANAYİ VE TİC. LTD. ŞTİ.
Tel: +90 232 254 29 17 Fax: +90 232 281 33 11
Web: www.maksanmutfak.com, e-mail: info@maksanmutfak.com

MASKOT MUTFAK EŞYALARI
Tel: +90 212 435 55 85 Fax: +90 212 435 42 58
Web: www.maskotmutfak.com, e-mail: info@maskotmutfak.com

MASTER MUTFAK CİHAZLARI
Tel: +90 212 485 85 30 Fax: + 90 212 485 85 34
Web: www.mastermutfak.com, Web: mastermutfak@mastermutfak.com

MAYAPAZ
Tel: +90 212 468 18 92 Fax: +90 212 476 21 58
Web: www.mayapaz.com.tr, e-mail: info@mayapaz.com.tr

MAYSA MADENİ EŞYA SANAYİ VE TİCARET LTD. ŞTİ.
Tel: +90 352 321 12 83 Fax: +90 352 321 12 00
Web: www.maysa.com.tr, e-mail: maysa@maysa.com.tr

MEGA MADENİ EV GEREÇLERİ
Tel: +90 258 251 69 90 Fax: +90 258 251 66 10
Web: www.boztepe.com, e-mail: info@boztepe.com

MEHTAP COOKWARE / Mehtap, Sms
Tel: +90 216 419 67 62 Fax: +90 216 419 67 64
Web: www.mehtap.com.tr, e-mail: info@mehtap.com.tr

MELTEM CUTLERY INC.
Tel: +90 212 642 32 86 Fax: +90 212 642 32 88
Web: www.meltemcatal.com.tr, e-mail: info@meltemcatal.com.tr

MELTEM-METİN EMAYE SAC SANAYİ VE TİCARET
Tel: +90 216 394 35 86 Fax: +90 216 394 35 92
Web: www.meltemgas.com, e-mail: sales@meltemgas.com

MERİH METAL INDUSTRY
Tel: +90 212 493 21 56 Fax: +90 212 567 75 80
Web: www.merihmetal.com.tr, e-mail: info@merihmetal.com.tr

MERT GIFT SHOP
Tel: +90 212 526 04 81 Fax: +90 212 526 04 81
Web: www.mertgift.com, e-mail: info@mertgift.com

MESSI EV VE MUTFAK EŞYALARI SAN.
Tel: +90 212 485 51 97 Fax: +90 212 485 51 98
Web: www.ardivasilver.com.tr
e-mail: info@ardivasilver.com

MEŞALE ÇAY OCAĞI KAZANLAR GIDA VE TEKSTİL SAN.
Tel: +90 212 418 00 00 Fax: +90 212 581 58 82
Web: www.mesale.com, e-mail: info@mesale.com

METE PLASTİK SANAYİ TİC.
Tel: +90 212 875 43 33 Fax: +90 212 875 33 03
Web: www.mete.com.tr, e-mail: meteplast@mete.com.tr

MİLENYUM METAL DIŞ TİC. VE SAN. LTD. ŞTİ
Tel: +90 352 311 44 54 Fax: +90 352 311 34 17
Web: www.palm.com.tr, e-mail: export@palm.com.tr

MİMAR SİNAN KITCHENWARE IND.
Tel: +90 212 422 90 94 Fax: +90 212 422 41 84
Web: www.mimarsinancelik.com,
e-mail: emine@mimarsinancelik.com

MİZAN EV GEREÇLERİ PLASTİK İNŞAAT LTD.ŞTİ.
Tel: +90 212 659 27 45 Fax: +90 212 659 27 03
Web: www.mizanplastic.com
e-mail: info@mizanplastic.com

HOUSEWARE · GIFTWARE · TABLEWARE · INDUSTRIAL · ELECTRICAL · PLASTICWARE · KITCHENWARE

MN-SKALA DEKORASYON
Tel: +90 312 349 02 95 Fax: +90 312 349 11 30
Web: www.deykimskala.com, e-mail: info@deykimskala.com

MONNA GLASS
Tel: +90 212 886 25 93 Fax: +90 212 886 25 97
Web: www.monnaglass.com, e-mail: info@monnaglass.com

MUTAŞ GROUP
Tel: +90 312 363 99 33 Fax: +90 312 363 94 92
Web: www.vitalmutfak.com, e-mail: info@vitalmutfak.com

MUTLU METAL SAN. VE TİC. A.Ş.
Tel: +90 232 853 74 44 Fax: +90 232 853 74 14
Web: www.mutlumetal.com.tr, e-mail: info@mutlumetal.com

MYTH ARTS
Tel: +90 212 249 09 53 Fax: +90 212 249 09 54
Web: www.myth.com.tr, e-mail: info@myth.com.tr

NARİN MADENİ EŞYA SAN. / Narin
Tel: +90 212 630 84 34 Fax: +90 212 550 38 15
Web: www.narinmetal.com, e-mail: ahunarin@narinmetal.com
info@narinmetal.com

NATSAN CO. LTD.
Tel: +90 212 605 02 65 Fax: +90 212 605 02 68
Web: www.natsan.com.tr, e-mail: info@natsan.com.tr

NATUREL DTM. MOB. SAN.
Tel: +90 352 322 20 25 Fax: +90 352 322 20 30
Web: www. naturelocak.com
e-mail: mali@naturelocak.com
mustafayayar@naturelocak.com

NDUSTRIO
Tel: +90 216 59302 42 Fax: +90 216 593 02 43
Web: www.ndustrio.com, e-mail: info@ndustrio.com

NECATİ ATLI-ATLI ÇELİK METAL SANAYİ
Tel: +90 344 236 08 51 Fax: +90 344 236 39 15
Web: www.atlicelik.com, e-mail: info@atlicelik.com

NEHİR MADENİ MUTFAK EŞYA SAN.
Tel: +90 212 656 65 50 Fax: +90 212 651 75 71
Web: www.nehir.com, e-mail: nehir@nehir.com.tr

NEPTÜN DIŞ TİC.A.Ş
Tel: +90 216 343 34 38 Fax: +90 216 334 93 79
Web: www.neptunev.com
e-mail: merve@neptunev.com - doruk@neptunev.com

NETLON MUTFAK ARAÇLARI / Netlon, Netlife
Tel: +90 212 270 44 91 Fax: +90 212 280 50 95
Web: www.netlon.com.tr, e-mail: bernay@netcelik.com.tr

NOUVAL GROUP MUTFAK EŞYALARI
Tel: +90 212 445 40 00 Fax: + 90 212 445 30 20
Web: www.nouvalgroup.com, e-mail: nouval@nouval.com.tr

OBJE PLASTİK TASARIM REKLAM ÜRÜNLERİ SAN.VE TİC.
Tel: +90 212 674 39 24 Fax: +90 212 567 52 34
Web: www.objeplastik.com
e-mail: info@objeplastik.com; sami@objeplastik.com

OĞUZHAN PLASTİK VE KALIP SAN.
Tel: +90 212 485 99 18 Fax: +90 212 485 99 52
Web: www.vialli.com.tr, e-mail: info@vialli.com.tr

OKYANUS MUTFAK EŞYALARI SAN. VE DIŞ TİC. LTD. ŞTİ.
Tel: +90 212 659 51 54 Fax: +90 212 659 56 10
Web: www.okyanushome.com, e-mail: info@okyanushome.com

**OMS KITCHENWARE LTD. / Oms, Didem, Oms Kitchen Star,
Oms Kinox, Oms Solingen**
Tel: +90 212 689 05 23 Fax: +90 212 689 05 97
Web: www.omscollection.com
e-mail: info@omscolection.com, aysun@omscolection.com

ONUR BAKALİT VE METAL SAN. TİC. A.Ş
Tel: +90 212 344 236 28 00 Fax: +90 212 344 236 28 05
Web: www.onurbakalit.com.tr, e-mail: veli@onurbakalit.com.tr

ONUR MADENİ EŞYA SAN. VE TİC. LTD. ŞTİ
Tel: +90 212 537 99 08 Fax: +90 212 617 91 63
e-mail: seliminci@onursteel.com

ORGAZ GAZ ALET. SAN. VE TİC. LTD. ŞTİ.
Tel: +90 216 593 93 93 Fax: +90 216 593 93 94
Web: www.orgaz.com.tr, e-mail: info@orgaz.com.tr

ORMEL OTEL RESTAURANT MUTFAK EKİPMANLARI SAN.
Tel: +90 212 321 01 02 Fax: +90 212 321 01 03
Web: www.ormel.com.tr, e-mail: ormel@ormel.com.tr

OS-KAR METAL SAN. TİC. LTD. ŞTİ.
Tel: +90 212 558 76 46 Fax: +90 212 558 76 56
Web: www.oscarsink.com, e-mail: oskarmetal@hotmail.com

OTTOMAN DIŞ TİC. VE MUTFAK GEREÇLERİ
Tel: +90 212 670 41 75 Fax: +90 212 670 48 84
Web: www.ottomanmutfak.com.tr, e-mail: info@ottomanmutfak.com

OTS METAL SAN. TİC. LTD.ŞTİ.
Tel: +90 212 613 80 30 Fax: +90 212 613 80 37
Web: www.otsmetal.com, e-mail: info@otsmetal.com

ÖDÜL MADENİ EŞYA SAN. TİC. VE LTD. ŞTİ.
Tel: +90 352 321 38 53 Fax: +90 352 321 38 52
Web: www.odul.com.tr, e-mail: yahsi@odul.com.tr

ÖNCÜ MUTFAK EŞYALARI SAN.TİC.LTD.ŞTİ.
Tel: +90 344 236 33 23 Fax: +90 344 236 03 49
Web: www.oncu.com.tr, e-mail: info@oncu.com.tr

ÖZAY TRAY CO.
Tel: +90 262 751 29 40 Fax: +90 262 751 18 79
Web: www.ozaytray.com.tr, e-mail: hdiktas@ozaytray.com

HOUSEWARE
GIFTWARE
TABLEWARE
INDUSTRIAL
ELECTRICAL
PLASTICWARE
KITCHENWARE

ÖZBİR METAL PASL. ÇELİK SAN. TİC. LTD. ŞTİ.
Tel: +90 212 615 54 13 Fax: +90 212 615 07 09
Web: www.ozbirmetal.com, e-mail: info@ozbirmetal.com

ÖZDEMİR KARDEŞLER KITCHEN EQUIPMENTS
Tel: +90 212 615 64 30 Fax: +90 212 615 07 09
Web: www.ozdemirkardesler.com
Contact: Turgut Özdemir, e-mail: info@ozdemirkardes.com.tr

ÖZGÜL MUTFAK EŞYALARI SAN.VE TİC.LTD.ŞTİ.
Tel: +90 344 236 64 00 Fax: +90 344 236 26 27
Web: www.ozgulmelamin.com., e-mail: info@ozgulmelamin.com.

ÖZ-ER PLASTİK SAN. VE TİC. LTD. ŞTİ.
Tel: +90 212 886 94 94 Fax: +90 212 886 94 96
Web: www.ozerplastik.com, e-mail: info@ozerplastik.com

ÖZMET A.Ş.
Tel: +90 212 886 88 00 Fax: +90 212 886 68 17
Web: www.oztiryakiler.com.tr, e-mail: ozmet@oztiryakiler.com.tr

ÖZMETAL STAINLESS STEEL IND. AND TRADE LTD. CO.
Tel: +90 212 547 44 71 (pbx) Fax: +90 212 558 76 46
Web: www.ozmetal.com.tr, e-mail: ozmetal@ozmetal.com.tr

ÖZMEN EMAYE SAN.
Tel: +90 352 321 35 51 Fax: +90 352 321 35 54
Web: www.ozmengroup.com.tr
e-mail: ozmen@ozmengroup.com

ÖZTİRYAKİLER METAL GOODS INDUSTRY/
equipmentsi Oven, Fryer, Gril, Cooker
Tel: 212 886 78 00 Fax: +90 212 886 78 09
Web: www.oztiryakiler.com.tr, e-mail: export@oztiryakiler.com.tr,
doztiryaki@oztiryakiler.com.tr

ÖZTİRYAKİLER PORSELEN A.Ş.
Tel: +90 212 886 88 00 Fax: +90 212 886 78 09
Web:www.oztiryakiler.com.tr, e-mail: oztiryakiler@oztiryakiler.com.tr

PAKSAN İÇ VE DIŞ TİC.
Tel: +90 212 519 06 01 / 528 00 53 Fax: +90 212 512 24 46
Web: www.paksan.info, e-mail: paksan@paksan.info

PAN MUTFAK EŞYALARI SAN.TİC.LTD.ŞTİ
Tel: +90 262 353 44 34 Fax: +90 262 353 45 69
Web: www.soli.com.tr, e-mail: rustem.zaloglu@soli.com.tr
info@soli.com.tr

PDS SAĞLIK VE GIDA EKİPMANLARI / Soft Bowl, Silicopan,Babysoft
Tel: +90 212 613 15 66 Fax: +90 212 612 71 95
Web: www.pds.com.tr, e-mail: info@pds.com.tr

PASDEKOR SÜSLEME VE DEKORASYON MALZ. SAN.
Tel: +90 212 235 11 11 Fax: +90 212 361 19 99
Web: www.pasdekor.com.tr,
e-mail:info@pasdekor.com.tr

PAŞABAHÇE / Paşabahçe, F&d, Denizli, Borcam
Tel: +90 212 350 50 50 Fax: +90 212 350 50 47
Web: www.pasabahce.com.tr,
e-mail: osagiroglu@sisecam.com
sucaliskan@sisecam.com

PİRGE - YEŞİLYAYLA CUTLERY TOOLS CO.
Tel: +90 224 216 01 02 Fax: +90 224 215 28 00
Web: www.pirge.com, e-mail: ömer@pirge.com
info@pirge.com

PLASBAK PLASTİK ENJEKSİYON VE KALIP SAN.TİC.LTD.ŞTİ.
Tel: +90 212 875 03 46 fax: +90 212 875 18 11
Web:www.plasbak.com, e-mail:info@plasbak.com

PORLAND PORSELEN SANAYİ
Tel: +90 262 648 59 00 Fax: +90 262 754 15 61
Web: www.porland.com.tr, e-mail: gebze@porland.com.tr

RENGA - MERCANLAR MUTFAK EŞYALARI SANAYİ / Renga, Tassar
Tel: +90 212 875 44 55 Fax: +90 212 876 67 42
Web: www.mercanlarkitchen.com, e-mail: export@ mercanlarkitchen.com

RİTİM HEDİYELİK VE AKSESUAR
Tel: +90 212 279 25 83 Fax: +90 212 279 34 49
Web: www.ritim.com.tr, e-mail: ritim@ritim.com.tr

ROSİTELL PLASTİC INDUSTRY
Tel: +90 236 214 01 03 Fax: +90 236 214 00 52
Web: www.rositell.com, e-mail: info@rositell.com

SAFLON METAL SANAYİ
Tel: +90 344 623 10 29 Fax: +90 344 623 10 29
Web: www.saflon.com, e-mail: info@saflon.com

SAM METAL TOKA
Tel: +90 212 549 87 22 Fax: +90 212 549 87 30
Web: www.sammetal.com, e-mail: hüseyin@sammetal.com.tr

SANİFOAM SÜNGER SAN. VE TİC. A.Ş.
Tel: +90 212 438 53 00 Fax: +90 212 438 53 53
Web: www.sanifoam.com.tr
e-mail: uyilmaz@sanifoam.com.tr, info@sanifoam.com.tr

SAREX ELEKTRİKLİ EV ALETLERİ
Tel: +90 212 471 11 11 Fax: +90 212 471 12 12
Web: www.sarex.gen.tr, e-mail: info@sarex.net

SAVAŞAN EMAYE VE SOBA SAN. / Grandeur
Tel: +90 332 334 05 50 Fax: +90 332 335 05 60
Web: www.savasan.com, e-mail: savasan@savasan.com

SELECT EV AKSESUARLARI SAN.VE TİC.LTD.ŞTİ.
Tel: +90 212 243 00 00 fax: +90 212 243 00 02
Web:www.select.com.tr, e-mail: seckinsaglam@select.com.tr

SEM PLASTİK SAN/ Sem, Sem E-Lite Plus
Tel: +90 212 736 07 37 Fax: +90 212 736 07 27
Web: www.semplastik.com.tr, e-mail: info@semplastik.com.tr

SENUR
Tel: +90 212 422 19 10 Fax: +90 212 422 09 29
Web: www.senur.com.tr
e-mail: serhan@senur.com.tr, info @senur.com.tr

SERKAN METAL SAN.
Tel: +90 212 689 40 44 Fax: +90 212 689 40 48
Web: www.camino.com.tr
e-mail: info@camino.com.tr

ACTFILE

SEVAL ALUMİNYUM BAKALİT ÇELİK PAZARLAMA VE SAN.TİC.LTD.ŞTİ.
Tel: +90 344 236 22 66 Fax: +90 344 236 05 39
Web: www.sevalcelik.com.tr, e-mail: info@sevalcelik.com.tr

SEYEKS DIŞ TİC.
Tel: +90 216 345 50 96 Fax: +90 216 337 17 46
Web: www.seyeks.com, e-mail: seyeks@seyeks.com

SGS MUTFAK EKİPMANLARI
Tel: +90 232 257 52 23 Fax: +90 232 257 53 03
Web: www.sgsoven.com, e-mail: info@sgsoven.com

SİDE ÇELİK
Tel: +90 344 236 44 55 Fax: +90 344 236 02 18
Web: www.sidecelik.com.tr, e-mail: info@sidecelik.com.tr

SILVER İÇ VE DIŞ TİC.A.Ş.
Tel: +90 352 241 01 90 Fax: +90 352 241 01 94
Web: www.silver.com.tr, e-mail: foreingtrade@silver.com.tr

SILVERLINE BUILT APPLIENCES
Tel: +90 212 484 48 00 Fax: +90 212 481 40 08
Web: www.silverlineappliances.com
e-mail: info@silverlineappliances.com

SINBO HOUSEHOLD APPLIENCES
Tel: +90 212 422 94 94
Web: www.sinbo.com.tr, e-mail: info@sinbo.com.tr

SNT TOPRAK ÜRÜNLERİ
Tel: +90 228 381 47 60 Fax: +90 228 381 43 26
Web: www.sntstoneware.com, e-mail: info@sntstoneware.com.tr

STAR MUTFAK VE MOBİLYA
Tel: +90 212 855 65 65 Fax: +90 212 855 68 70
Web: www.starax.com.tr, e-mail: info@staraksesuar.com.tr

STAR TEMİZLİK MAKİNALARI
Tel: +90 216 572 74 04 Fax: +90 216 572 92 25
Web: www.starmakina.com.tr, e-mail: star@starmakina.com.tr

SUN METAL
Tel: +90 212 475 99 66 Fax: +90 212 475 08 82
Web: www.sunmetal.net, e-mail: info@sunmetal.net

SUN PLASTIC HOUSEWARE / suncook, Sunday, Sunbath, Sunfix
Tel: +90 212 659 05 05 Fax: +90 212 659 59 60
Web: www.sunplastik.com.tr
e-mail: info@sunplastik.com.tr

ŞENİNOKS INDUSTRIAL
Tel: +90 212 221 15 95 Fax: +90 212 221 54 79
Web: www.seninoks.com, e-mail: info@seninoks.com

ŞENSOY MADENİ EŞYA VE KALIP SAN. TİC. LTD. ŞTİ.
Tel: +90 212 549 39 25 Fax: +90 212 549 15 16
Web: www.seden.com.tr,
e-mail: cansu@seden.com.tr, info@seden.com.tr

ŞENYAYLA PLS. SAN. VE TİC. A.Ş.
Tel: +90 212 514 16 93 Fax: +90 212 513 90 01
Web: www.senyayla.com, e-mail: senyayla@senyayla.com

ŞİRİN PLASTİK
Tel: +90 212 501 21 47 Fax: +90 212 577 54 96
Web: www.sirinplastik.com.tr, e-mail: info@sirinplastik.com.tr

TAÇ MUTFAK EŞYALARI/ Taç, Aksu,Vallena, Emprassa
Tel: +90 212 691 06 21 Fax: + 90 212 691 06 32
Web: www.tacmutfak.com, e-mail: info@tacmutfak.com

TAMLAS OTO LAS. MLZ. SAN. VE TİC. LTD. ŞTİ.
Tel: +90 352 694 51 76 Fax: +90 352 694 51 02
Web: www.tamlas.com.tr, e-mail: info@tamlas.com

TANTİTONİ (İnter Mutfak Eşyaları Tic. A.Ş.)
Tel: +90 212 293 02 93 Fax: +90 212 292 49 88
Web: www.tantitoni.com.tr, e-mail: info@intermutfak.com.tr

TAŞHAN MUTFAK
Tel: +90 212 683 00 69 Fax: +90 212 683 00 67
Web: www.tashanmutfak.com.tr, e-mail: info@tashanmutfak.com.tr

TEK-ART HEDİYELİK EŞYA
Tel: +90 216 433 33 00 Fax: +90 216 433 33 10
Web: www.tek-art.com.tr, e-mail: info@tek-art.com.tr

TEKA TEKNİK MUTFAK ALETLERİ
Tel: +90 212 886 95 00 34 Fax: +90 212 274 56 86
Web: www.teka.com, e-mail: cenk.cınar@teka.com.tr

TEKNO-TEL
Tel: +90 212 659 16 50 Fax: +90 212 659 17 53
Web: www.tekno-tel.com, e-mail: info@tekno-tel.com.tr

TEKNOGRAND SOĞUTMA SAN.
Tel: +90 212 299 68 64 Fax: +90 212 277 13 24
Web: www.teknogrand.com, e-mail: info@teknogrand.com

**TEKPLAS PLASTİK DAY. TÜK. MAL.
İTH.İHR.SAN.VE TİC.LTD.ŞTİ.**
Tel: +90 352 321 30 37 Fax: +90 352 321 30 38
Web: www.tekplas.com, e-mail: galaxy@tekplas.com

TEKSAN HOME APPLIANCES
Tel: +90 212 685 07 43 Fax: +90 212 685 29 50
Web: www.teksanevgerecleri.com
e-mail: teksan@teksanevgerecleri.com

TERMO GLASS IND.
Tel: +90 212 886 25 83 Fax: +90 212 886 25 88
Web: www.termocam.com, e-mail: export@termocam.com

TİTİZ PLASTİK DIŞ TİCARET
Tel: +90 212 798 24 90 Fax: +90 212 798 24 99
Web: www.titizplastik.com, e-mail: export@titizplastik.com

TOLKAR INDUSTRIAL CUANDRY & GARMENT / Tolkar, Smartex
Tel: +90 232 376 85 00 Fax: +90 232 376 76 58
Web: www.tolkar.com.tr
e-mail: info@tolkar.com.tr

TRINOKS EVYE METAL SAN. TİC. LTD. ŞTİ.
Tel: +90 212 486 39 12 Fax: +90 212 486 39 14
Web: www.trinoxevye.com
e-mail: y.asnas@trinoxevye.com

● HOUSEWARE
● GIFTWARE
● TABLEWARE
● INDUSTRIAL
● ELECTRICAL
● PLASTICWARE
● KITCHENWARE

Contact file

TURAN PLASTİK SAN. NAK. VE TİC. LTD. ŞTİ.
Tel: +90 462 711 43 61 Fax: +90 462 71143 62
Web: www.turanplastic.com.tr
e-mail: info@turanplastic.com

TUTKU METAL
Tel: +90 344 251 33 43 Fax: +90 344 251 33 29
Web: www.tutkumetal.com.tr, e-mail: info@tutkumetal.com

TÜRMAK MAKİNE
Tel: +90 212 281 51 04 Fax: +90 212 281 51 07
Web: www.turmak.com, e-mail: turmak@turmak.com.

UFUK METAL SAN.VE TİC. LTD.ŞTİ.
Tel: +90 344 236 01 30 Fax: +90 344 236 01 33
Web:www.ufukartglass.com, e-mail: uygar@ufukartglass.com
info@ufukartglass.com

UKINOX KITCHEN SYSTEMS INC.
Tel: +90 212 886 91 95 Fax: +90 212 886 91 95
Web: www.ukinox.com
e-mail: info@ukinox.com, export@ukinox.com,

ULUDAĞ MUTFAK SANAYİ
Tel: +90 224 256 62 32 Fax: +90 224 272 15 13
Web: www.uludagmutfak.com.tr
e-mail: info@uludagmutfak.com.tr

**ULUTAŞ METAL MUTFAK EŞYALARI
İNŞAAT SAN.VE TİC. A.Ş.**
Tel: +90 344 251 27 46 Fax: +90 344 251 27 45
e-mail: ulutascelik@hotmail.com

UTG DIŞ TİC
Tel: +90 232 441 41 90 Fax: +90 232 441 01 81
Web: www.ultratech.com.tr, e-mail: export@ultratech.com

ÜÇGEN INDUSTRIAL
Tel: +90 212 886 71 91 Fax: +90 212 886 71 94
Web: www.tribecafsp.com
e-mail: info@tribecafsp.com, taskin@tribecafsp.com

ÜÇSAN PLASTİK KALIP SANAYİ
Tel: +90 212 746 63 00 PBX. EXT NO: 115 Fax: +90 212 746 63 11
Web: www.ucsan.com.tr
e-mail: export@ucsan.com.tr

VARIŞ ISI SİSTEMLERİ
Tel: +90 362 266 53 22 Fax: +90 362 266 61 43
Web: www.varisltd.com.tr, e-mail: varissatis@varisltd.com.tr

VENTEKS DIŞ TİCARET LTD. ŞTİ.
Tel: +90 212 659 26 05 Fax: +90 212 659 26 08
Web: www.venteks.com.tr, e-mail: venteks@superonline.com

VIP OTEL EKİPMANLARI
Tel: +90 212 494 50 00 Fax: +90 212 494 50 03
Web: www.vipotelekp.com.tr
e-mail: info@vipotelekipmanlari.com

**VM BAKALİT METAL PLASTİK
MAKİNE İTH. İHR. SAN. VE TİC. LTD. ŞTİ.**
Tel: +90 344 236 24 24 Fax: +90 344 236 65 33
Web: www.vmbakalit.com, e-mail: veli@vmbakalit.com

WOODMARKT
Tel: +90 212 670 50 50 Fax: +90 212 670 50 00
Web: http://www.woodmarkt.com, e-mail: info@woodmarkt.com

YAŞAR TİCARET ENDÜSTRİYEL
Tel: +90 312 213 27 62 Fax: +90 312 213 00 35
Web: www.yasarticaret.com, e-mail: info@yasarticaret.com

YENİ SÜPER GAZ SAN.
Tel: +90 212 295 23 42 Fax: +90 212 295 23 43
Web: www.yenisupergaz.com, e-mail: info@yenisupergaz.com

YEŞİLLER/ Açelya, Serbas
Tel: +90 212 659 39 61 Fax: +90 212 659 39 60
Web: www.yesillerplastik.com, e-mail: info@yesillerplastik.com

YEŞİLTAN TURİZM VE MADENİ EŞYA
Tel: +90 212 746 56 56 Fax: +90 212 746 64 23
Web: www.yms.com.tr, e-mail: yesiltan@yesiltan.com.tr

YETKİN MFG. IMPORT&EXPORT INDUSTR
Tel: +90 212 671 22 46 Fax: +90 212 671 22 45
Web: www.yetkincelik.com, e-mail: info@yetkincelik.com

YILMAZ ATATEPE YILMAZ PLASTIC INC.
Tel: +90 212 564 51 00 03 Fax: +90 212 615 41 97
Web: www.yılmazplastic.com, e-mail: info@yılmazplastic.com

YILMAZ FIRÇA SAN. TİC. A.Ş.
Tel: +90 224 243 11 98 Fax: +90 224 243 16 36
Web: www.yfs.com.tr, e-mail: yfs@yfs.com.tr

YİBER ENGINEERING
Tel: +90 216 361 27 77 Fax: +90 216 361 25 26
Web: www.yiber.com, e-mail: info@yiber.com.tr

YNS DAY. TÜK. MAL. TİC. SAN.
Tel: +90 352 321 13 57 Fax: +90 352 321 13 59
Web: www.emerald.com, e-mail: izzet@emerald.com

YONCA LINES MUTFAK
Tel: +90 344 236 30 30 Fax: +90 344 236 46 24
Web: www.yoncametal.com
e-mail: info@yoncametal.com

YÖM-PLAST PLASTİK SANAYİ
Tel: +90 212 875 83 28 Fax: +90 212 875 83 31
Web: www.yomplast.com, e-mail: info@yomplast.com

ZAMBAK PLASTİK SAN.
Tel: +90 212 659 41 15 Fax: +90 212 659 42 90
Web: www.zambakplastik.com.tr, e-mail: export@zambakplastik.com.tr

ZİLAN DIŞ TİC. LTD.ŞTİ
Tel: +90 212 632 23 23 Fax: +90 212 589 63 28
Web: www.zilangroup.com, e-mail: info@zilangroup.com

ZÜMRÜT ART OF GLASS
Tel: +90 258 276 54 30 Fax: +90 258 276 54 99
Web: www.zumrutartofglass.com
e-mail: info@zumrutcam.com

This magazine may be ordered through booksellers or by contacting

iBooExport
"Reach the World "

Istanbul Office	London Office
EGS Business Park	3rd Floor
B2 Blok No: 12 D.01	86-90 Paul Street
Yesilkoy, Bakirkoy,	London
İstanbul 34149	EC2A 4NE
Turkey	United Kingdom
t: +90 850 460 1 064	t: +44 20 3828 7097

info@ibooexport.com II www.ibooexport.com

ISBN

978-1-947144-72-9 (sc)
978-1-947144-73-6 (e)

We care about the environment. This paper used in this publication is both acid-free and totally chlorine-free (TCF). It meets the minimum requirements of ANSI/NISO z39.48-1992 (r 1997)

Printed in the USA

www.ingramcontent.com/pod-product-compliance
Lightning Source LLC
Chambersburg PA
CBHW052348210326
41597CB00037B/6292